The New
REVOLUTION

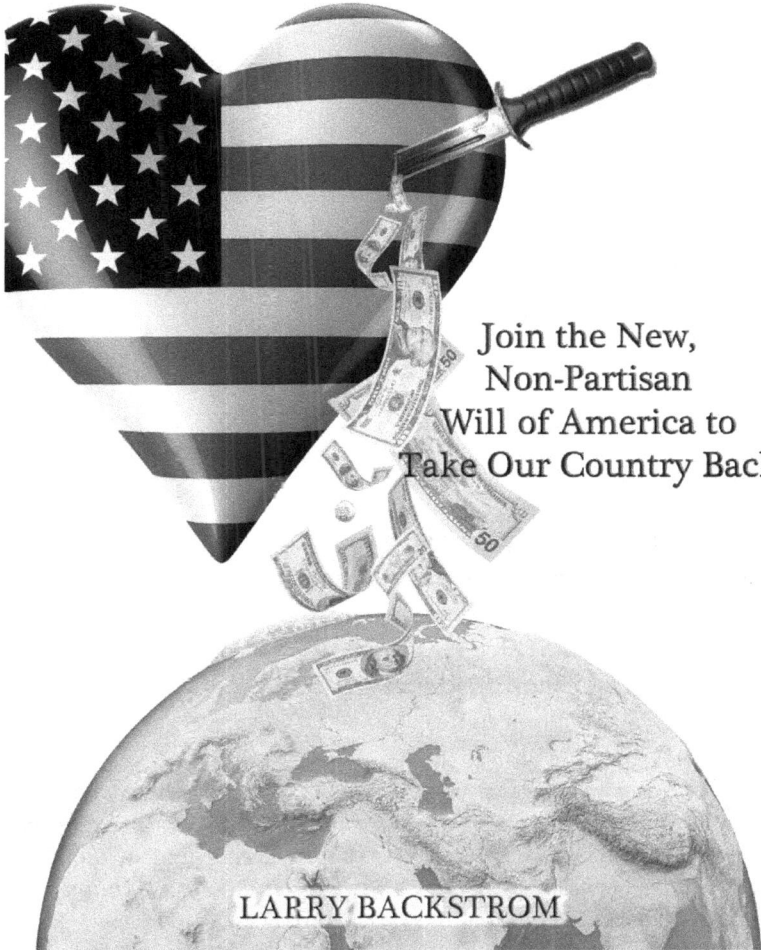

Join the New,
Non-Partisan
Will of America to
Take Our Country Back

LARRY BACKSTROM

Creative Force Press

Creative Force Press

The New Revolution
© 2015 by Larry Backstrom
www.thenewrevolution.website

This title is also available as an eBook. Visit
www.CreativeForcePress.com/titles for more information.

Published by Creative Force Press
4704 Pacific Ave, Suite C, Lacey, WA 98503
www.CreativeForcePress.com

ISBN: 978-1-939989-20-8

Printed in the United States of America

DEDICATION

I would like to dedicate this book to our wonderful planet that sustains us all and provides entertainment through her endless beauty and bounty of natural experiences.

May God bless us all and help us to mend her wounds that we, mankind, have created.

TABLE OF CONTENTS

INTRODUCTION

Why Write a Book?

I want to make it clear that by most standards I'm just a regular citizen of this country who sees a need for change. I am not famous, financially powerful or influential. I'm just one of the millions of people in America that you might call part of the moral majority or "working America." Frankly, the waste, greed and poor management of our country's money and affairs around the world is appalling, and I believe a large percentage of working Americans share that concern. So, this is why I decided to write *The New Revolution* – to share my perspective and offer solutions rather than to sit by, complain, and watch the sands of our prosperity erode systematically away.

In this book, many critical issues will be examined. Here are a few of the concerns I'll debate:

- War and military spending
- The environment
- Business regulations, rules, fees and taxes
- Poor, middle class and the rich
- Selection of leaders
- Privacy and our freedoms

- Moral deterioration
- Banks, financial systems and the deficit

Since the World Wars, a small handful of decision-makers order our young people off to foreign countries to fight. While I support our participation in the World Wars and I appreciate our soldiers, since that time to now, I believe our troops have fought mostly to protect large, corporate, financial interests around the world and to support the military war machine that has far too much power in our government.

My tax dollars would be better spent providing health insurance for the people and building better infrastructure in our country. Since when did our Constitution say that America was responsible to rebuild *other* countries? I do believe in helping other people, but if helping other people makes *us* sick, then why are we doing that? Also, where does it say in our Constitution to be the planet's police force? Are we doing the right thing letting our leaders build new nuclear attack submarines and refit 16,000 nuclear warheads with new firing mechanisms? Is this how we want to spend our money? No one has asked me.

What about the environment? It is a tremendous issue today, locally and around the world. The legitimacy of the science of global warming is a great debate raging amongst the parties. The evidence is clear: a crisis is looming for our planet and the next generations of our society. The health of our world and the planet needs to transcend all other issues. Our oceans and environment deserve the focus, not efforts to perpetuate war and conflict around the world. America would be wise to work with other world leaders now or we will soon find ourselves out of food, water and the ability to sustain ourselves.

For the past 34 years, I have been a businessman watching how complex our society has become. The endless sea of regulations, taxes and fees are now crippling our economy. Many of the rules and new regulations are well-intentioned to protect society in general. I can appreciate standards and safety. However, it's getting out of hand, and an inflationary bubble is about to burst.

Where does the money come from for compliance to all the regulations? Directly out of a business' profit, resulting in less job creation and lower revenues to spend. And, where does all the money *go* that's spent on regulation compliance? That may be the greater question.

The rabbit-like multiplication of regulations, rules and fees have come as a result of the political and judicial systems we've put into place. Our society has become increasingly complex and very difficult to navigate for the average individual. Business people across our country are often paralyzed by local building regulations and permit processes. Taxes and inflation are out of control. For example, when property values fall, county assessors lower property values on paper, yet increase the multiplication factor so their income stays the same. What? Deficit spending has become a habit with our legislators, while there are so many people being left behind; people with the ability and desire to work. Poverty is growing across our country – the division between the haves and the have not's continues to grow.

I have watched the family unit in America weaken and the people's belief in our leaders deteriorate. Patriotism is at an all-time low, while the support of our troops, by the people, is at an all-time high. The people are being flooded with propaganda and no one knows what to believe anymore. Finding the truth is often difficult in a world filled with special interests. Our young people tend to blindly believe whatever the media feeds them, not realizing manipulative agendas are often operating behind the headlines.

The term *free country* is no longer the whole truth. Does privacy still exist? Is there really freedom of speech in America? We as a society have put our faith, trust and money in the hands of our government. We have empowered them to defend and protect us and use our tax dollars for the benefit of the citizens of this country. Now, we are being spied upon by our own government (who is also spying on the entire planet).

God, faith and worship are being taken out of government and our educational institutions, causing the moral deterioration of our society and government. Our country was established by God-fearing people that made foundational decisions based upon strong, moral and biblical convictions. As our society is being led into an uncertain future, I am asking myself if we are, as a country, making the right decisions as we select our leaders. We have selected them, and they have brought us to our current circumstance.

I ask myself, and you, these questions. Complex questions make us think, and that is the purpose of this book. Join me in thinking things through. Perhaps by thinking a new thought we can make a difference in our country and our world.

Our Objective:

To take over our government with our ability to truly choose and vote. Send a message to our representatives that this is our country and our money by removing every single incumbent politician from office and staff our government with people who truly represent the people, not special-interest groups.

As I mentioned, I started writing simply to discover how I really felt about various issues in America. Now, I'm asking myself why we are evolving like we have. Are we where we want to be? Why have we, the people, allowed our country and economy to be taken over by special-interests and large corporations? We've become complacent and allowed ourselves to be ruled and divided by party interests. We have a large, corporate government run by special interest groups and big money, including the war-machine contractors. Writing has been a journey of questions and personal discovery, which I have broken down into topical segments to share with you.

We Can Do Something

In this book, there are many generalizations. Each topic of discussion has comments, and in some cases, suggestions regarding that subject. Some people might see this simply as a rant: an attack on the way of life of the greatest country in the world. I still agree that the U.S. is one of the greatest countries in our world. But without change, the unraveling will continue, and we will fall apart. We can do something to stop that.

Considering our population levels in the U.S. and the world as a whole, our old political systems do not work anymore. If we continue allowing two political parties and 535 people to control the affairs of 320 million people, we are fools. If the established system is so great, why is it not working well? If the parties can't agree, then let's find a new way to make our representatives work together for our benefit.

Chapter One

TAKING BACK OUR GOVERNMENT AND IMPACTING THE WORLD

The will of the people needs to reign again. We already have a peaceful way to determine our direction, and that is by unification with purpose and voting. Nobody wins a war. Nobody wins a fight, so there's no need for a violent revolution to get change. We just need a plan of targeted action.

Why? Every American deserves life, liberty, justice, opportunity, safety, and a voice. I believe every American voice should be heard when it comes to choosing the direction of our country. Let's take back our government!

What? The purpose is to take back our government by throwing out 100% of all incumbent representatives regardless of their party affiliation.

When? Start date is the next election, both local and federal.

How? Let us make it simple. Vote! And, vote with these goals in mind:

- Remove all incumbent candidates
- Candidates must be believers in God. They must truly believe they are running to serve the people, their country and the Creator.

- Balance the budget and work within the income of our government. No deficit spending allowed!

Who? Us! All citizens of our country must take this to heart and unite in order for this to work. We must send a clear message to the candidates that there will be no business as usual. They must be working on behalf of the citizens and not corporations.

Recently, I turned on the TV and was quite taken by the story of Benjamin Franklin. In addition to his brilliant inventions, I was inspired by his brave stance against England and how that helped shape America. Those were exciting times: breaking free from England and forming our own country. For early colonists being controlled from afar, taxes and governmental controls had gotten out of hand. With their ruling government an ocean away, there were many brave people who were not allowed to rule themselves and determine their own destiny. We had taxation without representation. This was a pivotal time in the development of what we now know as the United States of America.

Without a doubt, we are one of the greatest countries on earth. Like so many other countries with a powerful beginning, we're still evolving from the platform

> Are 'we the people' in control?

shaped during Franklin's time. Our Constitution, Bill of Rights and the Declaration of Independence are the foundation from which the people of America are to control the country. Notice I said *the people of America are to control the country…*

Through our electoral process, we determine our leaders, hoping their campaign promises develop into reality; a reality which would be in the best interest of the American people. We need men and women of strong character and wisdom; men like Franklin, who believed in God, which caused his actions and leadership to extend beyond selfish ambition and agendas.

Franklin made his declaration of faith six weeks before he died. He said, "Here is my creed, I believe in one God, Creator of the universe, that He governs it by His providence, that He ought to be worshipped, that the most acceptable service we render to Him is doing good to His other children, that the soul of man is immortal, and will be treated with justice in another life respecting its conduct in this one." Men like this were truly working with these strong moral beliefs for the best interest of the people.

What *is* the best interest of the people, and what is a satisfying life? Has it all gotten away from us? To take a real look at where we are today, we need to look at where we came from. Are *we the people* in control? That is an interesting question in itself. Is our representation working for us, or them? Who passes all these laws and invents all the new taxation? Does our current way of life fill each one of us with great joy? In the pursuit of happiness, have we found it? Will we ever find it? Do we really feel as free today as the mantra of our country would lead people to believe, or are we all slaves to a system run by big business and bankers? Take a step back and ask yourself: what is it that the world worships today?

From a very broad perspective, I would say, it's money that is worshipped! Has it not become most people's pursuit and desire? But, what has this pursuit of money brought us? Or, has it *bought* us? There's always a price to pay for that which we desire, and if the pursuit is money, the price is our human spirit and the health of the planet. It appears the whole planet is unified in its pursuit of money, but not in the evolution of the human spirit living in harmony with one another.

As our world has developed, along with it has come a precipitate of garbage – literally landfills full of waste and garbage tainting the planet that feeds and provides for us. Yes, we have hard-working conservation groups, but it is apparent that all of our efforts are falling considerably short. Why? Because cleanup and replenishment is not in the budget. Once again greed on every level of our society eats away at our collective home: the earth God gave us.

Let's stop kidding ourselves and admit we have big problems. The earth is heating up because of greenhouse gases and carbon dioxide levels. All around the world we are polluting our water supply with chemicals, our air with gases and our land with garbage. Are we doing better than two decades ago? I hope so, but we still have work to do.

> It appears we have enough money to wage wars around the planet, but not to clean it up.

We are also stripping the earth of trees, coal, fish, nutrients, minerals, oil, and gas. But, what are we putting back? It appears we have enough money to wage wars around the planet, but not to clean it up; not even in our homeland. How many more of these man-made disasters like the gulf oil spill or the nuclear disaster in Japan will it take to finally destroy our planet's ecosystems? All of this stems from greed. Who has the money and what are they doing with it? In general, it's not being used to clean, restore and heal.

Have You Opened Your Eyes?

I've lived a very fast 63 years on the planet, and have I learned anything yet? Yes! One important thing! I have learned about creation and the hand of God. I don't even know why we continue to teach Darwin's theory of evolution. The more our scientists know, the more we see the impossibility of all the species of life evolving from basic elements. What started out as one man's theory seems to have become a belief system in itself, requiring blind faith in impossible circumstances.

Now that science is getting a good look at the DNA helix, we see so clearly an intelligent design and can no longer deny a Creator; a Creator so great and magnificent that He is beyond our ability to comprehend Him and His gifts. Although I used to think evolution made sense, when I really looked around me, it started not to. I am now a Christian, and every day I open my eyes in awe of creation. If you aren't amazed everyday by the magnitude of the world around you, take time to slow down and think just for a few minutes about how lucky you are to be able to witness God's good works. Stop to consider the intoxicating scent of a flower, iridescent feathers on a bird, stunning sunsets, glittering constellations, and grains of sand. Above all that, *we* are His finest example of His work.

So, why are we here? We're here to learn that the greatest things in life are love, giving and forgiveness. If so, how are we doing with all of this? I say not so good...

Good Intentions

There are lots of good intentions out there, but we are

falling short. I won't dwell on the negatives, but let's first identify the problem before we can fix it.

We need a global awakening, and we can find it by taking a step back from this monetary madness to come up with a system by which we can all live in harmony on this planet. Is this where our leaders are taking us, and is this what they're working towards on our behalf? We have a shortage of good leaders who truly work on behalf of the good of all. Remember, we're just passing through.

When I stop and consider our society's skewed focus and priorities, I wonder why so many suffer in the world. Very few have great abundance and usually stand on the sidelines, doing nothing to help those in great need. None of us truly own anything here. We only have temporary custody of our possessions, and then we're gone. I try to keep this perspective, even though the pull of the *American dream* is ever present.

Here's a good question: how can we use our gifts and talents to help others around us? How many times have you and I turned on the TV and seen the shows about starving people or those in need of water, yet did nothing to help? Nobody wants to watch a mother holding a starving, dying baby in her arms. Why is one sixth of the world's population starving? We cannot deny these problems any longer. I am very upset, because through my years of living, I've learned to perceive others' pain and suffering. Some people make poor choices that cause their poverty, but some are born into bad circumstances and are at an extreme disadvantage from the start. Those people desperately need help from those more fortunate.

In order to change the spirit of the planet and heal it, we

need to change the way we measure success: by measuring the living standard of all people. This means we have to change the entire system of dealing with the resources God has given us, not exploiting them for just a few. We all know what is right and

> Change the way we measure success: by measuring the living standard of all people.

wrong. It's apparent when an individual or group twists the truth and justifies their bad behavior for their own purposes. We all intuitively know what adds value to others and what subtracts. This is one of the things we are here to learn. We can choose the light or darkness, stewardship or selfishness.

Some of our world leaders have even mistreated and exploited their own people. Giving these malicious, greedy leaders the boot is one of the steps I am talking about to make this world work for everyone. Usually a bad leader's reign starts with greed.

Greed

We've heard of the *haves* and the *have nots*, and we've seen the enchanting programs about the rich and famous. But, is it all for selfish gain? Shall we start asking the big philosophical questions about what these people, dynasties or companies are doing about global problems? Do they care? Although I'm not considerably wealthy myself, do I care adequately for those in need?

There are far too many individuals with extreme wealth that simply do nothing for others, and actually leave huge problems behind them. I don't want to state that *no one* is doing anything. There are many green companies with conservation programs working to replant, recycle and find new technologies. But, it is simply not enough. Perhaps we can divert some of the monies used for military programs toward planting seeds of prosperity for the misfortunate. And, it's not just the filthy rich or the government who should "do something" to help those in great need, I might add. That's up to you and me, too. We can still be greedy with our smaller amounts.

Greed also affects our environment. Our planet is crying black tears from the oil spills like blood flowing from our own bodies. She is raining acid and melting at the poles even now as I write. The ocean temperatures will cause aquatic life to die if we do not reverse global warming. Can we stop the competition and join the same team? We all want the same things: a quality life with love and to enjoy our time here on earth. So many people around the world are starving and impoverished, while others live in pure opulence and excess.

It's amazing how at times people have come together for a cause, like in 1985 when Michael Jackson, Quincy Jones, Kenny Rogers, and Tina Turner, along with a great group of famous artists recorded *We Are the World* during the African famine crisis. Wow, we were all in awe, admiring the great effort and collective consciousness of these great people. We need a similar effort today that spans the globe. Can we come together again for a good cause?

The World

Our world needs to come together right now. We need to end global competition and start taking care of the planet. Success is often defined solely in financial terms. "What were the profits?" is always the question. Let's redefine success as lifting the standard of living of all people, so that all may enjoy their life and contribute.

Each of us deserves food, shelter, education, healthcare, and freedom. We need to respect one another's individuality, but at the same time understand we all share the same planet, air, water, and similar life challenges. It is time to develop a unified philosophy of living and take care of the people *and* the planet, where everyone works with the common goal of planetary preservation. Let us keep in mind that when everything is measured on a financial basis, where there is competition, there is always a winner and a loser. No one wants to be the loser, so the competitive spirit.

Globally, we need to change the focus of our financial systems and social programs. When people start talking about social reforms, politicians start putting labels on philosophies like "socialism." Allow me make an important statement here about that. The largest socialist organization in the world is a *government*. Governments produce nothing, promote control, spend money, and each one takes very good care of itself. County, city, state and federal governments are supposed to be organizations that work on behalf of the people in their jurisdiction. However, it seems like they work more in the best interest of themselves and large business who control resources.

I say that our members of Congress are all socialists, both Democrats and Republicans alike. They all have their pensions, healthcare, vacations, and can vote themselves raises even when our national economy is failing. These leaders need to change the way productivity is viewed around the world and start a new program of reward based upon global unification and very strict financial reforms. *No one left behind* needs to be our new mantra and *love our planet* the swan song.

Along with flying our country's colors, what if we had a world flag with a picture of the planet on it as a reminder? Our marching orders need to start with the words LOVE and GOD! We each get one body and one world to live in. Let's honor and respect them both.

Division keeps us weak and mistrusting. We need to capture a spirit of global and philosophical unification, meaning a way of measuring and providing for the world's needs, both for business and personally.

Chapter Two

YESTERDAY

I find it very interesting when people talk about trends and project what might happen tomorrow based upon history. I have always found this to be absurd. Looking to history so as not to repeat mistakes is helpful, but each new day is unique unto itself. We've never been here before, and the circumstances have never been exactly the way they are now. There might be similarities, but each moment in all of our lives is unique, which is why life can be so exciting. That being said, in times past, there have been more troubled times for our nation's history, and other times more exciting for our people.

Looking back at yesterday only serves as a basis from which to view our current prosperity and gauge our progress as a nation. How do we stand today as people emotionally and economically? What is the mood of our nation today versus 60 years ago? How are leaders doing, and what is the true relationship between the American people and our current government? How are we doing economically, both locally and internationally?

Back in the 50's when my father and mother were starting their lives together, a man as a single-wage earner could support a family of 4 to 6 people. On a single income, he could purchase a home and all the things that went with it. We were in the post-war era when the economy was booming from the technological and industrial revolution that developed from the roots of WWII. What's happened since then, for the past 60 years, is crazy.

Today, I am sitting in my home office writing this book on a computer that didn't exist until the early 70's. I have to say that although there are many good things that have come from the computer revolution, it seems to have done three major things.

First, it's made the younger generation lazy and out of shape. The second result is that we're suffering from information overload that serves to stress most of us out. And third, our lives have been sped up in a technical way, taking us away from the natural world.

As children, we all played outside with our friends such games as hide and seek. We used sticks to play Zorro or walked around with a pillow case and played Superman. These games involved imagination, creativity, forming teams, running and jumping, digging and climbing. Today our children sit for endless hours in front of the computer and play games that involve killing and maiming the pseudo enemy. Although these games stimulate the imagination in some ways, our children's bodies are wasting away. They no longer seem to develop long term meaningful relationships. They are separated from one another and relate more to computers than to each other.

As young children growing up in the 50's, television was just becoming a household appliance, and the content and programing was just being developed. We had variety shows like *Ed Sullivan* and the first sitcoms like *I Love Lucy, Donna Reed* and *Father Knows Best*. We even had our horror films like *Frankenstein* or the *Werewolf*. Compared to today's movies, they would all be rated G, suitable for all audiences.

Everything today is about sex, death or war. There is far too much immoral drama being portrayed and it's forming the basis for societal behavior. Where is the control? There is none, relatively speaking, because there is no one home to model different behavior.

Where is Mom?

Back in the good ol' days, mom was there for us. Not just to see us off to school, but she was the very foundation from which our character was formed. She was the keeper of the home and the family, which we all know today is a very important job. During school in the 50's and 60's, we even had classes called *home economics* in which young people were taught the skills necessary to provide a good and healthy environment for their families. They learned skills like cooking and how to maintain a budget for the home.

My mother was the moral anchor and cheerleader for us children, and that was important to me. If I got hurt, I would come running and screaming for mom. After all, she provided the love and the nurturing I needed to feel safe and build my confidence. It wasn't just for us children either. She offered motivation and nurturing for my father, too, helping him stay the course and support our family.

People laugh when they think about the shows that depict the man coming home to his beautiful wife who would have his pipe, coffee, slippers, and the daily paper sitting next to his comfortable chair. He could smell dinner in the oven, which was almost ready, and the home looked neat and tidy. Now it seems like a fantasy to have someone at home taking care of all the background work so the man and the children can all be successful at work and school.

What happened to this little fantasy? Where is mom today? Who is taking care of the children? And, what is the mood of the American home/family today? What is the state of this American dream? Who can afford it? There are few families that can attain this dream, although we can obtain the material aspects of it if both adults in the family are working. Inflation has reduced the value of the dollar to one tenth of what it was worth just 35 years ago. Today, it's much less likely that a husband's salary alone can support his family's *American dream* needs.

So, where is mom? Mom is at work.

The American Dream

What is the American dream? We've all heard of the Cinderella complex: the woman being swept off her feet by the man of her dreams. They live happily ever after. Of course, they do the nesting thing and purchase the home of their dreams, settling down to have a family. They have to have all the possessions that will make their life complete: nice furniture, cars, maybe a boat. They have to paint the baby's room that certain color. These are the components of happiness – the things that make a life and a home complete in America, right? Let's not forget the TV, the "hi-fi" as my dad called it. With the industrial revolution booming during the 50's, TV had become a part of every American home.

> Is the American Dream really a nightmare?

The technological advancement in every aspect of American living soon hit the air waves and advertisements for every type of product was in your face on the TV. That fascinated America. We were told we all needed to have whatever cool, new product was being shown. This is the engine that drives our economy in America. Spark a dream or desire in the public, and they have to go out and buy it. Show it on TV, and America will buy it. Go to someone's home in America and it's filled with the things that are supposedly the keys to their happiness, and without them, they are seen as falling short and *un-cool*. The American dream.

As I look around my home, I realize that I've fallen into the same pattern. Things and more things – trying to find happiness and a sense of being complete. As a teenager living through the Vietnam War era, I became a non-conformist: completely anti-establishment, resisting all the ideals and established mainstream thinking about what makes a life complete. But, when a man falls in love, the nesting instinct takes over. As I began to settle down, it all changed.

I wanted to make my mate happy, and we started making our own nest. I finished my education and got that great job. I settled down into the *good life*. Each day, I'd come home and sit in front of the TV; that box that was always trying to sell me everything I could possibly think of. The next thing I knew, I became one of the great American consumers. I just had to have that new Buick and play golf with the new Arnold Palmer golf clubs. My wife just had to have that new Ethan Alan furniture. The next thing I knew when I looked around my home, it had become a collection of all the things that I thought would make me happy. My parents did it, and I am still doing it, but life in America is changing.

Capitalism is what's been driving America and the world for the past hundred years. Along with the growth of our economy and capitalism, something else insidious has been growing, too; the growth of *greed*.

There are two main types of greed: the greed for money and greed for power. Most people want to be successful and make money. In order to make money, we need to make profits. Owning a business and being in control has been a dream that's created massive growth in our economic engine in America. The achievement of the American dream has been the driving motivation for most of America. But, not everyone can make the same amounts of money. Even so, everyone wants to achieve a certain level of success and be able to have nice things in their homes. Business owners want to make the big money, but labor has organized to demand higher wages so their standard of living can be maintained. Truck drivers want to make the same amount as the business owners and the factory workers want to make the same amount as the truck drivers. And so, the politics of workers' rights and labor unions are born, and so is inflation.

Everyone wants a piece of prosperity. Even the politicians get into the act, standing up for certain groups of influence and creating departments within government to stand for workers' rights and regulations. And to think, it is all driven by the American dream! But, is the dream fading away?

Can all this continue at the current rate? All the demands of workers are pulling on businesses that are already in competition with one another. Businesses struggle for market share against one another, while trying to meet the demands of their workers and of the government. At the same time, inflation is increasing for all these reasons. The price of everything the American consumer needs to live keeps rising at an alarming rate. Just our basic requirements of food, gas, shelter, and healthcare are creating massive pressure on the home life of all Americans. The cost for goods has spun so far out of control. Why? Because every American demands to maintain the same standard of living that we call the American dream...

How can we all live the same lifestyle, have the same things, make the same amount of money, and stabilize the economy at the same time? How can housing prices keep going up and up, and then expect our young people coming out of college to be able to afford to purchase a home, especially when they can't always find a job? With the cost of healthcare going so out of sight, how can aging America ever afford to retire? I am beginning to think that owning a home and the ability to retire are going to become things of the past. They will simply become out of reach; things that only the most elite of society will be able to afford, because our money is becoming worthless.

Chapter Three

LEADERS, MORALITY
AND WHAT PEOPLE REALLY WANT

What does the average person in the world want? Let's consider what ordinary citizens are concerned with every day:

Got to make the house payment. Got to pay the property taxes. Why did the taxes go up again? Got to pay the income tax or the IRS will come after me. Got to have auto insurance, life insurance, homeowner's insurance, liability insurance, and contractor's insurance. Where are my insurance cards? Are my children and family safe? Do my kids have good schools? I've got to be educated, or bonded, or a member of a union or agency. Must pay my homeowners dues, water bill, phone bill, garbage bill, internet bill, sewer bill. Do I have the latest technology? My business isn't legitimate unless I'm a member of the local chamber, rotary, or my professional association. Can't forget the five food groups, 30 minutes of exercise, eight hours of sleep, and brushing my teeth twice a day…

These layers pile high on the emotional well-being of individuals in our society. People wonder why they can't keep their relationships and health together. Add the responsibilities of a family on top of all the everyday stuff, and no wonder people are stressed. Even people with great educations and a great track record can't find a job to fund this complicated web of existence. Yes, there are many people who take this stuff in stride and have gotten used to it, but it's all so crazy. We *can* do it, but should we?

When I wake up in the morning, do I think about being attacked by another country? Thankfully, no. I think about my friends and family. These are the basic issues we face. We want to have a home and something to eat. We all have our dignity and want to be respected, and we also want to have a sense of life purpose. This is where personal philosophy comes in. I believe that people don't mind working to earn their keep and don't mind contributing to the welfare of the community.

Got Joy?

I ask this question to you: do most people in America wake up each day feeling great joy in their lives?

Is life meant to be lived under pressure of performance? Every day Americans get up, go to work to try and make ends meet, and at the same time, accomplish some of their life's dreams. To some, this might mean having a family, and to others it might mean buying a new home or a car. This is what makes us all different. But, most people are feeling a lot of stress and pressure. Financial concerns are one of life's biggest stressors.

Once again, the tax structure in this country to support government, and the government entitlements are out of control because of big government spending. Where does the bulk of the money go that our families spend each year? It goes to federal tax, social security, the power companies that the government regulates, and all the other utilities like garbage, water, cable, and telephone. All these are regulated by government agency commissions that vote their own permission to take more from us based on the inflation that is largely being created by their increased regulations.

How would you like to be in charge of all the money? Sounds nice, doesn't it. You could vote yourself a pay increase and then charge your customers more money... because you feel like you need more. Is this the best behavior of a competitive, free and open market? If you feel the pressure at work of too much to do, you could simply decide to hire more people and increase taxes. I know this is an over simplification, but the process never seems to be fiscally responsible. Where does all of this lead us?

As I talk with my friends and family each day, it's not the work that we complain about, it's what's left over; the meager amount left after paying for the things we have to have, not to mention the things that are taken away from us. We all realize—because of the way our system works—the more you earn in this country, the more is taken away from you by our government on all levels.

For example, the way the healthcare system is today, most of the people in government don't feel the healthcare crunch for themselves. Why? It is an entitlement to them. They get it free or very low-cost. But, the small business person has to pay out of their own pocket for this ever-increasing cost, which has more than doubled in the past ten years. At the same time, the coverage (the actual health care and services you can have) has been reduced by 20%. Reduced coverage still leaves large liabilities with most of us after seeing doctors.

My monthly expenses are rising like a kangaroo leaping up a flight of stairs. Besides my healthcare cost woes, utility rates are now three times what they were just fifteen years ago. Have our salaries increased by this much in this timeframe?

Absolutely not. All this adds up to pressure on our existence. It can steal our joy, our sense of accomplishment and put our dreams out of reach.

I honestly believe that most people are dissatisfied with the way our government is being run today. We work way too much to support our government and have less time for enjoying our families and lives. Again, I have to ask, am I working for them, or are they working for me? We are the hardest working country in the world with the least amount of time off. Most people when we get to the end of our lives will say that about one another. He or she worked hard all their lives. But, did we live well? Did we live with great joy in our lives? Most people don't have time for that. I say it is time for significant change.

Time for Change

John Lennon wrote one of the greatest songs in the world, *Imagine*. I think he was one of the world's greatest philosophers, and he used his music to touch people. I believe his song *Imagine* should be the basis of the way the people of the world live their lives. Could we live as one? Can you imagine if all people lived in peace? Right now, that is not our reality. But, how could this become reality?

Imagine if there were no countries. What if it was just the *world*? A place where people lived and worked serving one another. It's a bizarre, wonderful thought, I know. But, what if?

Where does our current system go wrong? Isn't it by putting too much power in the hands of the very few? How often have we seen in our human history abuse and misuse of this power?

Let's look back through some history of great civilizations and leaders. We can start with Caesar, Napoleon, Hitler, Mussolini, Idi Amin, and Saddam Hussein. What do names like these have in common? Abuse of power! Even in our own country, if we take a closer look at history, we get a clearer picture of what took place. There are examples of this during administrations like Johnson (during the Vietnam era) and the G. W. Bush administration. We know that even in our own country, the land of the free, that our own government uses its power to manipulate the press and spread propaganda. The media is used to campaign for popular and political agendas.

I say it's time to re-write what we feel the role of big government is in our lives. Personally, I only need two things from government: protection and a national healthcare system. Let's eliminate all the duplication in our country.

Just Who is Representing You?

Most people in the world today have some type of faith and religious belief, and our nation was founded by people of the Christian faith. It is important to me that the leaders representing me believe in God and eternity. An atheist, for example, may believe there are really no consequences for behavior and may make decisions based on the belief that there are no relative long-term implications or repercussions. People with that perspective welcome short-sighted, self-serving laws that exclude morality, because in their opinion, morality is a non-issue.

I say, very simply, it is time to put faith back into our culture and insure our leaders are people of faith; faithful people who are doing things in the best interest of humanity *and* the kingdom of God (which also has the best interest of humanity). I want people who stand against the evil that exists in the world, who wi.. make decisions that are directed by God and His wisdom.

Leaders of Faith

We do not need people who would rule through violence and aggression, nor do we need leaders that would participate in genocide around the world. Even one unjust death is a tragedy. Our nation and every nation need leaders with the love of God and the value of life in their hearts to lead the world in healing.

Could the U.S. be the most influential country again, but in a different way? Can we get back to what made us so powerful and attractive in the first place? Faith, freedom, creativity, opportunity.

We need to love the world God gave us, including the people in it. Our leaders should want to lift up the hurting, hungry and the sick. We want those who want to restore the planet's environment and look for ways to continually preserve it. We want leaders who will raise the standard of living for everyone that is willing to work and participate in our society.

Our leaders need to have the right doctrine and love of humanity. The most effective leader understands he or she is following their calling from God to help others. They clearly know this is their life's purpose; a purpose beyond their own interests. When I look for a leader, I look for those who have wisdom, integrity, humility, and generosity.

Chapter Four

THE PARTY SYSTEM

If you're a member of an organization, you're going to promote its interests. Shouldn't the role of our legislators be to promote what is the best interest of the American people? When we have a divided system like we do, both sides are going to promote their interest in order to maintain power. So, isn't it obvious that the parties exist to maintain power in government by being able to manipulate who is being voted into power?

The way things stand now, the two major parties in our country have all the power and influence. They each raise money from those in the private sector who want to promote their interests. Companies, organizations and individuals give money to those who support their agendas and what they'd like to accomplish. What does it take to accomplish something? Money – government money for special programs!

When money is given to a candidate by an organization, it's only natural that the candidate will be influenced by that donation. This system is corrupt at its basic level. Why, after all these years, does this system still exist? This campaign donation system, coupled with the Electoral College, allows the parties and special interest to maintain and manipulate power.

Why would it be a requirement for someone to be affiliated in some way to a party, anyway? This is where the money comes in. This affiliation breeds corruption from the very beginning. I'd be interested in seeing a comprehensive list of where the campaign funds come from for each candidate. That would be a very revealing list. In order for this to be a system that expresses the will of the American people, it needs to have absolutely no special interest attached to it: no *"I owe yous"* to anyone but the American people.

When they say someone is being endorsed by the United Auto-Workers Union or the Teamsters, it really means they are connected to special interests and their money. It also means that person is expected to vote in favor of their issues when it comes to legislative issues. Special interest groups want *their guy* or *gal* in place to control the purse strings of the United States government's national budget. The people making these decisions fall on one side of the aisle or the other: Democrat or Republican.

> **Special interest groups want *their guy* or *gal* in place to control the purse strings.**

Let's eliminate the party system and establish a one-party system called the American Party, of which every citizen is a member. Let's allow qualified people to conduct campaigns, in a public platform, paid for by government funding, with no party affiliations. No private sector funding will be allowed. Every candidate gets equal time on network television as Public Service Announcements. Then, the people simply vote. Yes, just count the popular vote.

It seems so simple, doesn't it? Well it is, and it should be. Let's let the American people really vote. Aren't you tired of our money being wasted and spent on things that have nothing to do with taking care of us? I know that these suggested changes will meet with the most ferocious opposition you've ever seen. Our legislators would be outraged that anyone would promote such a thing. They love the system. Heck, they *are* the system! Everyone currently in power in the system would be outraged, but not the American people.

It's not that our newly-elected representatives wouldn't disagree from time to time, but it would be more about straightening up issues and creating collaborative solutions, not conforming to party platforms. People would still be liberal or conservative, but with no party affiliation or influence. People would come together on issues, not on a party name.

Campaigns and Fund-Raising

During the 2008 presidential election, it did not seem to be about who was the best man or woman for the job, but instead it seemed to be a war of the parties: Democrats and Republicans. This struggle is for gaining control as *decision-maker* of the world's most powerful economy and military machine. Our election process does not make any sense at all anymore. What is it that drives these parties? Money, of course! Why do we even have these divisive parties any longer? It appears to be a way for the government to control who gets to stay in power. Do we, the people, really have choices in this process? I would prefer a broad spectrum of choice, but what is offered to us is extremely narrow.

The reasoning behind the party system lies in where the money comes from and who backs the candidates. The parties determine who the American people ultimately get to vote for, but before that, it's the money and the caucus system that determines who gets to run. So, here is this great sham: the American people don't determine anything, really. It's all in the hands of the big money and the super delegates.

I would like to call the American people together to vote out all party-affiliated candidates (of both parties) in order to completely clean house. It would be most effective if it's done on a federal and local level.

Let's send a message to government that we want our money spent on us! Your dynasty is over!

Since you cannot solve the partisan bickering, we'll get rid of it. We don't want someone to represent a *party*, we want someone to represent us, *the people*.

I say during the next U.S. election, not a single party candidate should be voted for. Understand, I know that there are some really great people in Congress, but that's no longer the point. The point is that we don't want people from the right or the left side of the aisle. In fact we want no aisle at all

> **We don't want people from the right or the left side of the aisle. In fact we want no aisle at all.**

and desperately need radical spending changes.

As long as the parties stay in control, you and I have no real choice! So, you want to get on the ticket and run? In order for that to be possible today you'd need to have tremendous financial backing from special interest groups. You'd also need to be connected to the main parties and their sources of funding. Then, there's the endorsements and the screwball delegate system to consider. Oh, and don't forget you'll also need to be connected to the media that covers the candidates and spreads the word across America's great propaganda network. Don't think for one minute that the media doesn't support parties and agendas. It's all about influence; influencing opinions towards party agendas.

Most of America thinks that the primaries determine who runs on the party tickets. No, it's actually the caucuses that determine who runs on the ticket. Unless you attend and vote at a caucus, your vote in the primary determines nothing. Is this all in the best interest of the American people? It's all a big show – smoke and mirrors, manipulating of power at the highest levels of government.

What about all the other smaller parties and the way the campaigns are run? I say that if special interests want to contribute to the national elections of candidates, then let them contribute to a pool from which all candidates draw their funds. All candidates should get all their money from the same place, giving no regard to anything other than if they're qualified to run for office. The networks should do the right thing and cover all participants on an equal basis. Why not eliminate the party and financial influence on the candidates and distribute the campaign money equally, letting the American people do the voting?

Unaffiliated

What if our candidates had no party affiliation at all? What if they stood on their own, declaring their own solutions, opinions and beliefs and were purely supported by the people who believed in that platform? The party system really only allows that group of people to control who we get to choose from! Why do the parties determine who my options are? The parties are influenced by so many special interest groups who reach in with their money. Whichever party serves their self-seeking purposes is who they support, persuade, and then pressure. Their main concern is which party controls federal money and programs that affect their interests and regions of the country.

And, what is this business of caucuses and super-delegates? Why has the power been taken away from the people? Whose idea was it to allow a handful of people called "super delegates" to control who we get to vote for? Who are these people, anyway? Do they share my views? Once again, we need to make sure these representatives are people of faith who are genuinely acting on behalf of the people.

Get Rid of It

While writing this book, Barak Obama is in his second term as President. He was elected twice under a mantra of "change." History is now showing that the people of America want change; changes like I am writing about in this book. In 2008, we had our first inauguration of an African-American president. Wow! I am so pleased that the people of this country have embraced a willingness for diversity in our leaders. Real change is possible, and for me, this was a glimmer of hope.

Certain mindsets changed, but unfortunately this presidency has proven to be no different in creating real change in other areas. I have never in my life time seen such legislative gridlock. The parties stand in complete opposition to one another's proposals, lobbing hateful sentiments, and nothing productive is getting done.

Many of our leaders have criticisms, but offer no suggestions about the changes that can make a real difference to the overall welfare of the majority of the people of this country. The only way to really fix the problem is to get rid of the people causing the gridlock. When change comes, it means we are going to be operating differently. There will be some special interest groups that won't be happy. Too bad. It might mean the total collapse of some types of businesses that are now negatively affecting the quality of life for the majority of American people. Sometimes businesses fail. These things happen.

Yes, you guessed it: I have some suggestions, and they may sound a bit radical. Even so, I think they need to be seriously considered.

We need to ask some fundamental questions about each of these areas and see if they are a true benefit to our society. So, let's make a little list and see how this feels to most people.

The special interest *get rid of* list:

- Lobbyist organizations
- Party system
- Special government retirement programs
- Healthcare and insurance providers
- The Electoral College
- Campaign fundraising and donations
- The banking system

We've already discussed the party system, so in the next chapters, let's explore each of these other areas and ask ourselves how (*if*) they benefit us in our society. Keep in mind that for our discussion, I am talking about benefiting the *majority* of the American people.

Chapter Five

GET RID OF SPECIAL INTERESTS

As we move toward a global economy, should we be legislating laws, delegating spending and creating regulations directly for small special interest groups? Doesn't this keep us from being competitive globally?

Let's think more about where we are financially in relation to other countries. It isn't difficult to see that our standard of living is much higher than most. Other countries compete for the work and win because their standards and rules are different (although truthfully, in some cases, inadequate). Their economics are not generally plagued by special interest groups.

In my perspective, the big question here is has our government enabled foreign competition by passing protective legislation for special interest groups, including their own? The answer is absolutely, yes. This trend needs to somehow be reversed.

In this chapter, various special interest groups that I believe should be eliminated will be discussed. Let's see if you agree.

Lobbyist Organizations

I believe this is one of the greatest points of organized theft in our country: lobbyist organizations.

Special interest is an interesting term. The lobbyist reminds me of the old TV program *Let's Make A Deal!* Why should the various industries be allowed to influence the people responsible for representing the American people? Name any industry, and there will be some lobbyist pushing to promote legislation that's in the best interest of that group. They want their agenda pushed. The group that most needs a lobbyist pushing for them is *the American people.* What is *my* special interest as an American citizen?

> **The group that most needs a lobbyist pushing for them is *the American people.***

Barak Obama made a campaign promise to restrict access to our elected officials. Hmmm...I don't think it has worked. So, what would happen if we had an all-out restriction on Capitol Hill? Would the House and Senate then be acting on behalf of majority of Americans and *their* best interests? Think of what would happen to major control groups in our country and what affect it would have on technological development.

For example, notice how big oil has kept energy's technological development stifled. People have invented many alternative ways of fueling cars, but where are all those options? Electric cars have become available, yet not widely used. It's easy to see how oil's financial influence has affected what should be a free market system. By now we should all be driving electric, solar, hydrogen, or some kind of hybrid car, and the switch probably should have come 20 years ago.

Why shouldn't special interest groups have to compete in the free market like the rest of us do in business? We have special protection in the form of legislation that protects organized labor in the public bid area. What about the relationships between the oil industry, the automobile industry, Capitol Hill, and Wall Street?

Not only have we lost our competitive edge around the world, but we've allowed these companies to perpetuate their thievery. We can't fix automobile companies by giving them money any more than the banking industry. Our whole economy runs off small, innovative business. Their tax revenues support government on every level. These are the financially-productive, responsible companies that pay their taxes and debts. The bailouts our government offered were not voted on by the American people. We allowed these industries to come into our government and promote their needs.

Again, I go back to the idea of nationalizing the banks. Isn't that what is already happening in a sense, by allowing the auto manufacturers to borrow directly from the government? So, why couldn't the people do that and eliminate the irresponsible people in the middle who ran their companies into financial problems to begin with? These people are effectively lobbyists for their own special interest. This is no different than military contractors and contractors, such as Warburton.

We can go on and on discussing government money being funneled into special interests (drug companies, tobacco, medical, insurance, Hollywood, etc.). They all promote "protectionist" legislation and development money for their own industries. Protectionist legislation protects the big guys (e.g. companies, agencies and entities) and their interests, but often to the detriment of individual citizens. This should not be the role of government to listen to their interests. Our government's role should be the safety, security and welfare of American families and individuals.

The Party System

Do the people have control? Looking at the big picture, we see the party system: Democrats and Republicans. It is very interesting that these parties are supposed to represent different lines of thinking, encompassing every option and solution there could possibly be. They end up being more like the Hatfields and the McCoys: two camps warring one another.

We as Americans are supposed to fall into one of the two categories, wearing one label or the other, but never both (or neither, for that matter). I sure wish things were that simple. There is no way that we can look at the many issues we're faced with today and simply dump them into a category group for that group of leaders to take care of it all.

Frankly, it looks to me like the party system only serves to *divide our country*. What is the real party system purpose, if not to unite us? The real purpose is to maintain the power control base in our country.

My thoughts on the party system deserve more attention, and I'll return to this topic later in the book.

Special Government Retirement Programs

Presidents, those in Congress, our Supreme Court Justices, and many other government workers have their own pension system. Why don't they use Social Security like the rest of us? It is *our* government! The people's government!

Why should federal employees have a different program than ours? Why should they have special entitlements that *we* have to pay for? They are lucky we gave them a job! Are they serving us, or are we serving them?

The people who own businesses in this country don't have retirement systems with the benefits that federal employees do. In fact, we do not have any retirement program other than something we research, create and manage for ourselves. We also don't have the healthcare insurance paid for us like government officials do.

Healthcare and Insurance Providers

Do we have a good healthcare system in America? Although we have many good, dedicated people working in healthcare, no, we do not! Once upon a time things were simpler, but our system has grown into its current condition because (again) of special interest. What is in the best interest of the people? A national healthcare program that protects all its citizens (not extended to illegal immigrants).

If we're spending the bulk of our nation's income on the military, we have no money left to keep our nation healthy. It's time to shake it up, and that means getting rid of insurance companies. If you look around, in every community, you will find huge, ivory towers built by the insurance companies who keep denying claims, raising rates and increasing our deductibles. Make no mistake – these are *for-profit* companies.

Why do the Canadians only pay about $125 a month per person for their national healthcare program and we pay about $450 per month per person? What is happening to all the money the insurance companies are collecting? Have you ever heard about any insurance companies going bankrupt in

> **We have no money left to keep our nation healthy.**

America? Never.

Why should an American citizen who has worked all their life be bankrupted because they need an operation? This government is supposed to be for all the people! Why should government workers on every level get the finest insurance (that is paid for by the small business people's taxes) when the small business people themselves can't afford the same insurance we're providing for them? It is purely wrong! Are we working for the government or vice versa? Government agencies are supposed to be working in the best interest of the American people, not themselves.

> **Is the government working for us or vice versa?**

Recently, Obama tried to pass the single-payer healthcare plan for the American people, and the insurance lobbyists won the battle. It only took six months after that for the insurance companies to raise their rates between 35-40%. Due to that change, my monthly rate with United Healthcare went from $412 to $593. Our deductible went up to $2000 per year, and they added a new $250 per year deductible for prescriptions. We are paying all this money to an insurance company which will only pay a maximum of 80% of the bill for any major healthcare problem. I am now 63 years old, and at this rate what is insurance going to cost in another 10 years when I am over 70? I just can't imagine.

Here again, healthcare is another area where middle class families have to worry about special interests influencing our nation's decision-makers. One of the reasons people elected Barak Obama was because of his campaign promises to restrict lobbyist access to our Congressmen and Senators in DC.

Electoral College

This is an outdated system that has nothing to do with the will of the American people. Why should a smaller group of people have a larger influence with their votes? Who are these people? It is just wrong!

When George Bush won the election in 2000, Al Gore won the popular vote. Although Republicans were thrilled, it was a violation of the greater will of the American people. If we have the computer technology to do our secure banking online, we could certainly vote online, and the popular vote wins. We are one country, after all. Yes, we have state representatives in the highest levels of government, but that is for legislative issues, not voting on national campaigns.

Let's just keep it simple and honest. Electoral College, you need to finally graduate and move on.

Campaign Fundraising and Donations

When you receive money from someone, they expect you to either support them in their way of thinking or by promoting their agenda. What happens when a labor union supports a candidate for office? Do you think they would expect you to oppose their union? No…they'd expect you to look favorably upon them. You cannot have someone freely acting on behalf of the American people when they're being supported financially by a group of organizations expecting support.

How do we get from where we are now to where we need to be? Stop the fund-raising and allow qualified candidates to run for office in a non-partisan, publicly-funded campaign.

Banks

Finally, we come to discussing the banking system's special interests. This one deserves a whole chapter of its own. See more in chapter five.

More Commentary

Special interest groups will always exist in the world, because everyone has some sort of agenda. But, the level of influence these people have on our legislators is outrageous. Why are we still letting special interest groups and lobbyist run this country? I say *goodbye* and *good riddance*.

To have any type of recovery, we'll no doubt step on some toes. Some people won't be happy. In fact, we all have some special interests of our own. A good example is Social Security. As we age, we become very protective of that program.

> **Vultures soar over Capitol Hill, ready to pick the bones of the economy.**

Take a look at who's hanging around Capitol Hill. They're like vultures soaring over the body, ready to pick the bones of the economy. We have to ask ourselves again if what's going on in this *good-ol'-boy* atmosphere is good for the majority of the people in America. Remember, we are a capitalist society, and everyone is looking to get their piece of the pie.

Why in the world should the American people have to bail out the very people who've stolen our wealth through deceptive tactics? Who is represented by the special interest in Washington? Do you think that the insurance companies want a real, national healthcare program? Do you think that the banking system wants to nationalize the banking systems? Do you think attorneys want to eliminate the automotive insurance industry? None of these groups want this, because it would take them out of the flow! They would have to find a new way to make a living. Why does our system have to stay the way it has always been?

Get the lobbyists out of Washington, and let the government do what helps Main Street America. Let us borrow our own money to start a business. Make it affordable to purchase a home again. Take away foolish requirements for insurance coverage. And here's a thought: build a national system for car insurance through taxing each gallon of gasoline purchased. If you drive more, you pay more to cover your insurance costs. There are lots of creative ideas we can collectively come up with to make the U.S. more competitive around the world and at home. It's inevitable that someone is going to be unhappy with changes though – lobbyists for sure!

Life on the Farm

I have to appreciate my adolescent years being raised on the farm. I think it was one of the times in my life that made me most appreciate God's creation and the natural way of things. One of the things you can't help but notice is the cycle of life and the rebirth of all the life forms on the planet. When spring arrives each year we see the sprouts of the leaves on the trees, the grass start to grow again and the spring flowers and bulbs coming back.

We had sheep, cows, dogs, horses, cats and lots of chickens. As a young man I watched the animals in the acts of natural procreation. There is nothing sick or perverted about it, it is just God's natural way of things. There are male and female: nature and procreation requires a male and female.

I would like to state that **I have no issue with the, LGBT community** and their choice to love or live with someone of the same sex. I have and have had gay and lesbian friends throughout my life. It is their private business and should remain that way. I once read a book about Edgar Casey, and he explained being attracted to the same sex by saying a spirit is either male or female and sometimes a predominantly male spirit is born into a female body or visa-versa. That made a lot of sense to me! I also feel that who we carry on our health care insurance etc., should also be our private business and not be yoked to the definition of marriage.

Here is my true concern. Our recent high court ruling regarding marriage will change how the rest of the world views America, *and* considering that 96% of the US population is heterosexual, once again this is a special interest question that's affecting all of America.

The LGBT (gay, lesbian, bisexual or trans-gendered) community (or special interest group) has been doing a very effective job over the past decade of promoting their agenda. Somehow, we've been coaxed down a path to believe marriage has a new definition—a new look that the majority of Americans will never participate in—and anyone who doesn't support it gets labeled cruel and unusual…or at least "unprogressive." I'm all for progression, but this feels like we just got a flat tire.

I was blessed being raised as a country boy that learned what it is like to really be in touch with nature and see the natural way of things. I think that city life has had a lot to do with our society's metamorphosis. Now many people live so far away from the natural life God planned for us.

The US Supreme Court recently voted to legalize same-sex marriage on a national level. The vote was 5 to 4, in favor. This decision is about a lot of different things besides equal rights for same sex couples. I believe that this decision will change the way other counties view America.

My main concern is, again, the power that special interest groups have on legislation. In my research, I found a recent survey revealing that approximately 3.8% of the U.S. population is LGBT. At less than 4% of our population, this clearly is a special interest group that has pushed their agenda. I really think issues like this should stay out of politics and never should have made it to the Supreme Court. We appointed and elected people to represent the will of the majority of Americans, correct?

Gay marriage clearly does not reflect the overall life style of this country, and it's just another example of decisions being made *for us*. This very small percentage of the population has somehow taken hold of our political system and twisted our laws to perpetuate their own special interests. We are now being taken for a ride.

I would further bet that if the American people voted on this issue instead of the Supreme Court decreeing a decision, results would have been roughly 90% against and 10% for the measure. Do we not get a say in an important social issue like this? If our will as "we the people" is the principle thing, then both sides of any issue deserves a voice and the opportunity to vote.

So, my questions would be these: from what perspective are we viewing the responsibilities of our high court? Are they not working on behalf of the American people? Should they be voting in a manner that reflects the feeling of the majority of American citizens? Or, if they're voting according to the Constitution and its allowances, why are they redefining social and moral issues that the Constitution does not discuss?

Legislative Costs of Special Interest

If you want to do some building development, be prepared to confront government bureaucracy all the way! A law has been passed that says you can't get a building permit unless you have a stamped set of plans from a licensed architect. But, architects are not engineers, so if there are any load bearing structures, you also need an engineering stamp from a structural engineer…and if you have special electrical needs, you need to have an electrical engineer create a panel schedule before your plans can be reviewed.

These plans will be reviewed by a member of the city or county responsible for that area where the building is taking place. The plans examiners are generally members of the International Conference of Building Officials (ICBO). All of these groups have lobbied for protectionist legislation that says you can't get a permit unless each of these groups has gotten their piece of the pie. As a result of their lobbying, the International Building Code and various state and local legislation has been created to protect these groups.

I believe that very often, the end results of building safety are much better and normally the intentions of these groups are good. However, what does this do to the building community? There are so many layers involved that it's no wonder that someone can't build a new business and support the cost of the facility that houses it.

Why are the permit fees from a city more than the cost of

an entire home 60 years ago? Those fees support the government, which is nothing more than a special interest group that's counter-productive to our society! If an architect designs a building and gets all the appropriate engineering from all the appropriate certified engineers, why do we have to pay the cities to review his work? If his work is faulty, he will be out of business and his business insurance will take care of it.

Why do these thick layers show up in government rather than the private sector? Yes, let's have accountability. Accountability is good. Let the professionals create the project, let the builders build, and have it inspected by people who know what they're doing. Shouldn't the builder be responsible for doing the work and knowing the codes? Shouldn't the architect know all the codes, too? Let's peel away the overlapped layers and simplify the system with some level of accountability.

The same is true with all the duplication in our government's federal and local agencies. Why do we have so much duplication? It only adds unnecessary expense, time and frustration. We need to take the burden off of the private sector and allow it to breathe.

This is just one example of the ridiculous amount of layers that legislation has created, which is a stop gap to productivity. What about the countless unions, drug companies, insurance companies, lawyers, military contractors, medical providers, and bankers? The amount of legislation they've collectively lobbied for is mind boggling. Who can navigate thru all of this extensive legislation that special interest groups have pushed for? They get what they want, and we get confused and overwhelmed.

Chapter Six

THE BANKING INDUSTRY

My father taught me that the only thing that really matters in a man's life is integrity. I know he left out a few other important details, but this was one of his hot buttons. His wisdom was right, and it helped me develop a sense of pride from always having paid my bills on time and as promised. I have now been a business owner for 29 years, and throughout that period of time, I have been involved in many banking contracts including loans for real property, vehicles, credit lines and homes.

My brother and I were business partners for 25 years, and I handled most of the banking and business side of the company. He was a field man, working the construction side of our business. Both of us felt it was important to maintain a long-term relationship with a bank, and at the same time develop a reputation of having credibility. I found out that is nothing but a bunch of B___ S___! I cannot tell you how crushed I was when I found out that our long-term banking relationship meant nothing to the bank at all, except profits!

I Thought They Loved Me

Back in 1986, our bank was a small community bank that handled our deposits and checking accounts. We started by funding the purchase of our service trucks. We had a small fleet of four trucks and technicians that went out and repaired commercial food service equipment. We decided to open a sales division in 1987 and applied for a $1000 credit line. We would use the credit line to purchase equipment from the factories. We would purchase the equipment, ship it to the customer and bill the customer on account. We would cycle the line as the money came in.

Our good payment history allowed us to soon acquire a $5000 line, then $10,000, then $50,000, and finally up to $250,000. We also purchased some commercial land and then built a building for our company in the year 2000. On a personal note in 2007, I purchased two lots to build some homes overlooking the Puget Sound, and the Olympic Mountains. But, more on that story later…

All of this we did with the same bank until 2009. This is when reality struck me, hard!

It turns out that our bank had invested very heavily in Fanny Mae and Freddie Mac. Their stock went from $100 per share down to $1 per share overnight. The FDIC immediately took over the bank and auctioned it off to another bank from the East Coast. All the local players remained the same, but they changed all the rules.

First, after giving me the money to purchase the lots to build my houses, and promising me they would fund the project, they cancelled my funding and stuck me with a 9.5% interest-only payment at $2700 per month on a $300,000 loan. They would not renegotiate the interest rate, and I was very upset. I had perfect credit with this bank and had borrowed millions of dollars over the years building casinos, country clubs, schools, and prisons, paying my payments faithfully. By now the entire housing market was crashing across the country, and not a single bank would entertainment the thought of funding this housing project. I was forced to go to my personal investments and retirement funds and pay off this loan. I never would have purchased the land had I known they would pull out! Six weeks later, I received a payoff on a large project and walked into the same bank and paid off my credit line which was up to $175,000 at the time.

Over a six-week period I had paid this bank off two loans totaling over $475,000 and did not owe them a dime! One week later, they sent in an account representative and pulled my credit line from me entirely. They actually cut off the only major source of funding I had for my business projects. Without money, you cannot make money. You have heard it said, "You need money to make money!" This same bank went through our community and pulled the credit lines of over 60 small businesses with no regard for their well-being and with no rational justification. They said *they were no longer in that business*. My question is…what is the purpose of a bank if not to support small business and families in the community? Shameful.

I was shocked and devastated. This meant I had to change the way I did business entirely. Once again, I was forced to go to my personal savings and fund my own business. Had I not been a saver and long-term thinker, I would have gone out of business due to the lack of operating capital. I spent the next five years working out creative ways to fund projects with my customers. Perfect credit scores, loyalty, and long-term relationships mean nothing to banks anymore. Banks are businesses that borrow money from the Fed and lend it to *you and me*! They are about profits, and if you happen to fit the criteria, you may be able to do business, but only on *their* terms! My emotional attachment to my bank and the loyalty I thought they had toward a good customer like me was pure fantasy!

> **They didn't love me, they just loved profiting from me.**

It turns out they didn't love me, they just loved my money when it was convenient for them.

Thomas Jefferson was Smart

In light of the present financial crisis, it's interesting to read what Thomas Jefferson said about the banking system in 1802 – two centuries ago.

"Banking institutions are more dangerous to our liberties than standing armies. If the American people ever allow private banks to control the issue of their currency, first by inflation, then by deflation, the banks and corporations that will grow up around the banks will deprive the people of all property until their children wake-up homeless on the continent their fathers conquered."

Britain is currently in the process of nationalizing their banking system. I would advocate this position for the U.S. as well, and have the middle-man profits generated by the bankers eliminated on loans, both domestic and commercial.

Our country went away from the gold standard in the early 1900's, when a cartel of powerful bankers convinced Congress to print money based upon the loan portfolios of the largest banks in the world. JP Morgan was one of the main benefactors of this plan. As a result, the Federal Reserve was born, spawned from ideas formed by this cartel at a secret meeting held on Jekyll Island off the coast of Georgia. Jekyll – a fitting name for this two-faced plan. The goal of the banking community was, and has always been, to enslave America in debt as they rake in the interest payments. Sadly, they have done a real fine job.

Why would Congress authorize and implement this? Because of the kickback they receive called the *prime rate*. The bankers simply offered a bribe to the government, and we got another hidden tax. They charge us interest for our home loans and the prime rate portion of the interest goes back to the Fed. They split the profits from lending us our own money! Whose money is this? It is our money, and why should the banking industry be allowed to make such huge profits from our labor to own a home? This has been the most counterproductive move in our country's history. It literally has put this group of companies in control of all our wealth and property.

The Fed loans the money to the banking system based upon their asset base. Banks literally double the cost of money coming from the Fed. Now, banks are allowed to borrow 20 times their asset base due to banking deregulation. Does it make sense to allow them to borrow 20 times their own ability to pay the money back—borrowing it from us…the people—and then make huge profits for just a handful of bankers?

Why, if a person is a qualified buyer for a home, should they have to pay 2.2 times the purchase price of the home (over 30 years) to a lender? Think about it. We are borrowing our own money. Why shouldn't a qualified buyer be able to purchase a home from the Fed directly at the discount rate/prime rate?

Sure, the banks provide a service facilitating the loan process, but give them a one-time fee for it instead of 30 years' worth of interest. That's an enormous burden. The risk of us borrowing at the discount rate is not any greater, and the bank can't pay the money back either if someone defaults. We have lent banks so much money that the Fed can't afford to let banks fail. Heard about the saying, *too big to fail*? This is the reason. We've given them too much control over our money and the housing and commercial real estate markets.

Now, with so many failing mortgages and foreclosures, both commercial and domestic, we see the Fed bailing out the banks through short sale programs. Short sales literally steal wealth from middle-class Americans. How? When they short sell a house in your neighborhood, values are lowered for everyone else's, too.

Why should the bank (over the life of the loan) make (in interest payments) more than the initial cost of the home? As a result, not many people end up actually ever owning the home they live in. They go from mortgage to mortgage, having only the masquerade of home ownership. I am in favor of capitalism, but only to a point. Once it reaches the point when people are slaves to lenders, *that* is a problem.

I think every person should be able to feel secure in their home, never feeling like their personal safety is in jeopardy. Why not just get dollar-for-dollar loans from the government, paying them back with no interest, or at just one or two percent? If you have a job, you should qualify on some level relative to your income, and instead of the bankers having all this extra income, that extra money could stay in the economy to purchase other goods and services.

Anyone who is in business needs loans from time to time, and it's easy to see that the local market is being controlled by banks. If we ask about rates on a loan to purchase property, we would find it set at the same rate at every local bank. The same is pretty much true with credit lines and construction loans. The local bankers all know each other and have a fix on their profits.

Think of what it would mean to our economy if we were able to borrow money at one or two percent interest. There are two good reasons to eliminate the middle man for home loans secured by the property itself: increasing the purchasing power of consumers and fueling the housing market again. It would also allow home owners to pay off loans quicker, which would mean more cash would be available to spend in the retail market on consumer goods.

There would be many other legitimate benefits from handling money this way that would affect the quality of life for middle class America. The principal advantage is more money in the pockets of the people. Pure capitalists love this idea, and socialists might call this a form of *redistribution of wealth*, but I would call it *wise*. Stopping the banks' special interest group from stealing from American home buyers (in a federally organized program that makes us pay 2.2 times the market value of a home) only makes sense.

Let us not forget that the money we are borrowing is *our own* money to begin with. Why should we allow a handful of people to fleece the American people? We are being ripped off!

Why Bail Out the Banks?

The U.S. is deeply involved in the international money market, and the value of our dollar on the world market is based upon our national balance sheet (which shows our national assets and liabilities). This balance sheet shows all the loans made to banks by the Federal Reserve as an asset. Because of loans showing as an asset, if we allow the banks to fail, it immediately causes the devaluation of U.S. currency. At this point, the Fed has to print more money to keep the banks from failing or our economy will be bankrupt. Frankly, if we really want to get the economy going again, we need to free up money for the people to spend on goods and services provided by businesses.

Unfortunately, we're gridlocked with mortgage loans and credit card debt to banks. Remember the housing market and mortgage crisis that hit a few years ago? What happened, you wonder? The banks and their greed caused the inflation in the housing market. Against all previous best practices, people were allowed to borrow up to 125% of the appraised value of the home they were purchasing. The arrangement between the appraisers and the banks helped people over-borrow against homes, which for a short time stimulated our economy. But then, the fallout inevitably came.

Whose fault was this? It was the Fed and the bankers' fault! But, ill-informed consumers bought into their scheme. It was great to take a loan out on your equity, get cash and then buy a new car or furniture for your home. Why not take a vacation and pay for it over the next 25 years on your home loan! No problem that the loan was secured by your home which has become only half of what you borrowed against it. If the bank and their appraiser said your house was worth $250,000 and they lent you $250,000 shouldn't the bank and the appraiser have some liability? Now the house appraises for only $175,000. Why should the bank expect you to continue to pay more than the house is worth? Did they not create the problem by offering irresponsible loans (which caused a rash of foreclosures) and also short-selling the neighbor's house and dragging down the values in the market for all the nearby homes? This is a new problem and big banking is right in the middle of it, yet *they* are the ones being bailed out? Who is it that represents the American people? Who is allowing this to happen?

Young people can no longer afford the American dream. The bankers in this country drove the housing market out of reach for those who needed starter homes. Entry-level prices became far too high! If no one can come in at the bottom, then no one else can move up to the next level. Could we reset the entire housing market? But how? Allow the banks to short sell all the repossessed properties and have the Fed print the money to make up the difference on the failed loans so the federal loans to the banks won't fail. This way, banks stay solvent…but people are homeless! This is what's really happening, being done with our money! It also causes the value of existing homes all across America to drop back 30% or more.

> Young people can no longer afford the American Dream.

Is this a purposeful, systematic stealing of the equity from the American people to benefit a handful of bankers? This housing crisis also caused rapid inflation to the dollar, increasing the national debt and in turn, devaluing our dollar.

Why should we give all this money to the banks who use it to take *more* from the American people? They have proved themselves untrustworthy. It is our money, so why couldn't we just forgive all the home loans across America (on a certain level) and let the American people put their monthly income back into the economy? Why did the government choose to bail out the banks instead of the people that lost their homes? Is this special interest at work again?

Years ago, I knew a family who emigrated to the U.S. from Russia. They told me an interesting story. When the Russian economy collapsed several decades ago, a majority of the people lived in government-owned housing. To get the economy going, they simply told each household that they now owned the home they were living in. Although this might have some inequities in the plan, it would do two things for the U.S. economy: free up income to spend for other goods and services, and free up money to be lent to business from the banking community. The banks can disclose all mortgages, and the government could choose to either forgive the related debt or give the bankers the money. In turn, this second option would mean bankers could lend it once again to small and large businesses. Including mortgages on commercial buildings in this debt forgiveness would free up operating capital to spend on capital equipment and expansion.

I was curious to know how many home owners with mortgages are upside down on their mortgages, so I investigated on the internet. It turns out that one in five homeowners owe more than their home is worth if they were to sell. Why should someone continue to pay on a home mortgage that is higher than the market value of the property? Some would say, "It's the risk they took buying the home." Sure, there's a certain amount of risk when it comes to investing, but buying a home? I say the banks manipulated their position with Congress, because the banks ultimately owe the money to the Fed. If the Fed does not get it repaid, the economy fails. If the banks don't get the money to lend, their profits fail. Keep in mind, whose money is it?

Again, this is a really sweet deal for bankers. Why did we relax the lending regulations so that banks were allowed to lend at 20 times their asset base? No individual or business would ever get a deal like that. Normally, I can get a loan for an amount that's about 35% of my net worth. Banks borrow the money from the American people and charge us interest; an amount of interest that adds up to over twice what we agreed to pay for the house in the first place. This is no longer the American dream – it's the bankers' dream. I thought our country was *of* the people *by* the people and *for* the people...not financial institutions. Who is winning here, and who is losing?

The latest in banking is now to charge us for taking our own money out of the bank when using a debit card. This is our money they want to charge us to take out...what?!

Oh banks, how I do not love thee...let me count the ways...

Chapter Seven

TAXES, FEES, INFLATION AND CRAZY REGULATIONS

I enjoy telling the story of the first new car I purchased. It was a 1973 Chevrolet El Camino: brand new and pale yellow with real chrome bumpers. I paid $5300 for it, and proudly drove it off the lot...right over to the general tire dealer and had brand new mags and fat, 60-series tires put on it. Next, I took it over to Midas and had new glass-pack mufflers put on her. She was a real car. The total cost was $5600. Today, if they still made the El Camino, I would bet the car would sell for around $35,000, not including my special upgrades. This would be a factor of 7 times what it cost just 35 years ago.

When I reminisce, I distinctly remember one of the first gasoline shortages in 1979. Let's call it the "so called" gasoline shortage. Gasoline was about .55 cents a gallon at the time, and now it's 7 times that. A good pair of Levis sold for $5. They didn't even have designer jeans back then. Levis *were* the designer jeans, and today they are around $35 a pair. Designer jeans can be $90 to $190 a pair, depending on the market and brand name. Cigarettes were always about the same as a gallon of gas, about .50 cents a pack. Now they're almost $7 per pack. In half my lifetime, I've seen nearly everything increase in price by a factor of 7x or more.

It was 1974 when I purchased my first home in California's Bay Area. I bought a home that was built during the time Woodrow Wilson was in the White House. Strangely, when I did a remodel several years later, I found a news-

> I've seen prices for everything increase by a factor of 7x or more.

paper stapled inside the walls from 1920. There was an article from the San Jose Mercury News about Woodrow Wilson's daughter. But, I digress...

I paid $17,000 for that home, and my house payment was $125 per month back in 1974. I was 24 years old. Since then, the San Jose/Bay Area has become one of the most expensive real estate markets in the US. Recently, that same home in San Jose sold for $950,000, and it has not changed much. That is 55 times what I paid for it. Today, if I purchase a similar home in Washington State where I currently live, it would sell for at least $225,000. Using that more reasonable number, it is still about 13 times more than housing costs earlier in my lifetime.

These numbers just don't work anymore. The American dream of home ownership is slipping away from many. What about our children?

My daughter is now 30 years old, and the medium-priced home in our area is about $250,000. With taxes, principal and interest, she would pay around $1700 a month for that home. With the average, two-person income in America being about $70,000 per year, is the American dream available to this group of people? This is the very root of the housing market problem. People can no longer afford to come into the market at the bottom. The bottom isn't low enough. The income is not there.

So, although trends aren't always predictable for the future, let's just say that in another 35 years, we'll be conservative and estimate that the medium home will go up another ten times. That home would sell for $2.2 million dollars (if it were in my area of Washington). The bank would require a 25% down payment ($550,000) and the payments would be about $17,000 per month. What? Keep in mind that this is an 1100 square foot, two bedroom, one bath home built in 1920. Why, oh why, have things gotten so out of control, and where will they go from here?

All Down the Line, Tax Everything You Can Think Of

In America, what makes our economic system run? It is simple: our system starts with the motivation to be successful by a few individuals who venture out to run their own businesses. Sixty percent of all people employed in America work in small businesses of ten employees or less. It starts here on the front lines with a brave individual (or individuals) who want to make their lives better than it would be if they were working for someone else. So often, many of these people have a dream, but no idea what they are getting into and what it takes to run a small business in America today.

It doesn't take long before they find out about all the laws, regulations and the tax structure that supports the government's income needs. This is where everything becomes so complex that the average individual gives up rather than trying to navigate their way through our various government systems in order to be financially productive.

The first discovery is that people find out they don't actually own anything. Local government rules are in charge, and we only take temporary custody of something for the purposes of business or temporary occupancy. Then, they find that they need to be given permission by our government to do anything to their property. Some months ago, my neighbor got in a lot of trouble with the city for cutting down trees in her yard…on her property. If you want to cut down trees on your land, you need a permit and have to pay for the permit. This is a small example, but it goes much deeper than that – much, much deeper. Who gave the government this power? They gave it to themselves.

While the government is collecting our tax dollars, what is it that they are doing with them? Wouldn't you think they would be improving our roads, building our schools and building more parks? Evidently, there is just not enough money in the budget for that. It is now the responsibility of the citizen who wants to build a home or business to pay for the sidewalks, street lights, storm drainage, and sewer lines, and don't forget the permits and fees for each of those items. Then, once you've paid for and built these extra items that you won't ultimately own, you'll hopefully be given permission to go ahead with *your* project. How crazy does it get?

Private Property?

Recently, I attended a pre-submission conference in a county office regarding the development of a commercial site for a restaurant. We all gathered around a conference table like you would at Thanksgiving, and I had a thought about giving thanks at that moment. I wondered if the government is thankful for us giving them the money they need to sustain their families?

The property owner, myself (food service consultant), the civil engineer, the architect, the structural engineer, the landscape architect, the mechanical engineer, and the owner all sat on one side of the table. The other side of the table had all the county experts: the Fire Marshall, the Urban Forester, the Environmental Biologist, the Building Plans Examiner, and the Traffic Control Manager. We were ready to find out all about what the county wanted in order for us to be given permission to build on the owner's property. Mind you, it's the owner's land...

Introductions were made around the table like during the coin toss at the start of a playoff game. After the introductions, the development services manager for the county starts in with his list. We were briskly taking notes. Of course, you cannot do any development unless you first have a stamped set of plans from a professional licensed engineer for every aspect of a project. You can't even imagine the expense involved in obtaining these drawings from each of the people involved. I noticed that as we moved around the table, that even the so-called *experts* needed to check with someone else regarding some of our questions. This is an indication that they don't even know all of their own rules. Most of these rules are outlined in the new international building code...no one could possibly know all these absurd rules. And, not knowing the right questions to ask up front can turn around to bite a land owner later in the process.

As the meeting continued, the list grew of what the owner was going to need to provide to get the permits. Sidewalks, storm drainage, street lights, sewer lines, road frontage, fire hydrants, bike lanes, and of course the geological studies. As we moved through the oppositions lists, I was taking my notes and smiling until we hit the environmental biologist's analysis and the study regarding the habitat for the Western Pocket Gopher. I started laughing and the manager asked me if I had a comment to make. I said, "Why yes, I do." At which time I made the clicking sound you would hear while putting a shell in the chamber of a shotgun while hunting. Everyone started laughing, but it's not funny. They were actually requiring the owner to hire professional people to do these studies and turn in the results to them prior to any further development work. If they find even one gopher, his dream is done!

He also can't have a permit unless he has provided a ten-year, environmentally-safe pest control plan for the area. He needed to provide a federal traffic impact analysis to determine the impact the development of his project would have on the pattern of traffic all the way from the nearest freeway. All the while, he still does not have any idea if they will *ever* grant him a permit for his project. He just wants to open a restaurant to use his skills, serve the community and make a profit.

I went around the room and added up the development costs for the plans for the restaurant, *not* including any costs to actually build his building, parking lot, or the required "improvements." The total was over $150,000 *before* getting approval for his project. What if he spent that on planning and it was ultimately denied? In addition, the owner had to pay for the permits which cost around $100,000. This included the cost to hook up to the sewer they have to pay to put in, which they will then be billed for monthly, along with the water. Add to this the cost of all the other things like sidewalks, sewer, street lights, fire hydrants, bike lanes, and storm drainage, and you have to ask yourself what happens to our tax dollars?

What do you call this? Are these just another form of taxes? A sidewalk has become a tax, a permit is a tax. They even charged him for the meeting itself! The owner is a young man and his wife, and his father owns a couple of existing restaurants, so they have a general idea of what to expect…but do they really?

Let's say this nice young couple gets a loan from the bank. They have no idea how many agencies are lining up to tie into their business. This is only the beginning of a never-ending path of regulations, entitlements of government and charges by utility agencies. The path to their success is full of well-crafted obstacles, something which most private sector people don't really understand!

The Cost of Compliance

This hasn't been my only experience with the craziness of building and property development. A few years back, I was so excited to finally pay off my house. I was single at the time, and was able to put enough money aside to pay off my home early. My accountant advised me that I would be better off if I had some type of write-offs for taxes, so I started thinking about building my dream home. I decided that I wanted to find a circumstance where I could build two homes and sell one to make some extra money, and then sell my current home and pay off the mortgage on the new one. These are great ideas in theory, but the reality was a nightmare!

I called my realtor friend, Phyllis, and started the search. I finally found a couple of vacant lots in Olympia, Washington, up on a hill, overlooking the city and the Puget Sound.

The thought of having a home in that location with a

beautiful view of the water and the Olympic Mountains got me really excited. I immediately called my banker and took him and the bank's vice president up to the lots and told them about my ideas. They both committed to supporting the financing for the project and the land purchase that day. Once again, I felt that 20 years of banking history with them really meant something. All I had to do was put my home up as collateral for the loan. As it turns out, that was the dumbest business move of my life. I had no idea what a bumpy road I was about to go down to try and build these homes.

I went ahead and made an offer on the lots for $65,000 *less* than they were listed for, and to my surprise the owner accepted. Now I know why! I called an architect friend that had worked on several school projects with me, and I trusted him. I hired him and a civil engineering firm and then scheduled a pre-submission conference with the City of Olympia. I soon learned that every city has what's called a *comprehensive plan*. Cities actually dictate exactly what type of development can be done in every section of town.

I could not believe how convoluted things became. I had to pay the City $1000 to have this 2-hour meeting. Around the table they had the Fire Marshall, the Urban Forester, the City Project Manager, and the Plans Examiner. We had preliminary plans for two townhouse buildings (for a total of four dwellings), and they simply said that the plans were not feasible. A little more help for $1000 would have been appreciated, but they did offer some information: visit our website to view the rules for compliance for building in the City of Olympia. Great.

They informed us that once we had a plan that complied with all the rules, we had to submit the completed set of plans in quarter-inch scale in triplicate. The complete set needed to include civil engineering, structural engineering, landscape plans, and architectural renderings of the finished product in color for their review board. They wanted full-frontage improvements (improvements made to the road in front of my property which I didn't own) including, storm drainage, a street light and a 200-foot ribbon sidewalk that ran from my property up along the neighbor's house to the next street. In addition to that, they wanted $26,000 per house as a "City Development Fee."

Keep in mind that there was no sewer on the street in front of these lots, and apparently we needed to also somehow include this as a part of our development.

This meeting did not go well. The next submission that was made by my civil engineering firm was laughed at by the city plans examiner who commented that the plans were not done by anyone who had knowledge of what it would take to build in the city jurisdiction. The engineering firm charged me $26,000 for a set of plans that the city would not approve; plans that were not buildable. Why would I pay for plans that were engineered incorrectly and rejected? So, I objected and they put a lean on the property, forcing me to hire a dispute resolution mediator who negotiated the release of the lien for a negotiated amount. I ended up hiring another firm and instantly got the plans approved by the city…conditionally.

This all took a year and a half. By this time, the real estate market had gone in the toilet. We actually had several meetings with the city along the way, after changing firms, and they still never offered any advice that would lead us the short way thru the permit process. I honestly felt they were trying to discourage me from the project. They were not in any way servant-hearted or helpful.

By the time we finally got conditional approval, my bank had been taken over by the FDIC and sold to another bank back east. The new owner denied the construction loan and stuck me with an interest-only 9.5% loan on $300,000. I now had property I could not develop and had to make payments on during the worst real estate disaster in our nation's recent history.

The city was unwilling to help with any of the infrastructure development. We had to clear the property, put in a tree tract which had to be shown on the landscape plans we were required to submit with the construction plans. We had to put in a grinder pump sewage system which included digging through a right-of-way to make the sewer connections. We had to bury the electrical cabling, bring in the water pipes, and pay for a new fire hydrant. We also had to put in sidewalks, storm drainage and a street light. And, for all of this we also had to pay the $26,000 permit fee per house. Total cost of property, frontage improvement, tree tract, sidewalks and civil engineering came to $438,000. That is $219,000 per lot. It used to be straightforward: you buy the land, hire a well-driller, make some feasible plans, and put in a septic. Not so anymore!

I only want to illustrate this for you so you clearly understand the potential pitfalls of property ownership. Just because you purchase something does not mean the powers that be will allow you to do anything you want with it (or anything at all in some cases). As a matter of fact, you are not allowed to remove trees or dig or build without the permission from the city. You do, however, have to pay taxes to the county for the property, whether you do anything with it or not. Then, you have to pay to comply, and this does not guarantee you can do it cost-effectively.

The level of frustration that a project like this could bring a person with an idea is staggering. Why am I required to improve property that I don't own? Why is the process so difficult, even when my plans were (finally) feasible? So, do we own anything? What rights does a person actually have as a property owner?

Cities and other municipalities have created development services departments which are designed as revenue generators. This is another way to generate profits to perpetuate their entitlements which the average American worker does not have. If you think you actually own something you are living in a fantasy. Does it really pay to take these risks as an entrepreneur in our world today?

You used to be able to hire an architect and let them be responsible for the project, and then a contractor would build it. They were responsible for their own work and liable for any inadequacies. Instead, this became a trend across the country and has turned into a business. These fees and new building regulations are pushing development costs beyond reasonable levels. These are the type of things that put home ownership beyond the reach of the average working American today! For me this was a very expensive lesson in life. So where do we go from here? A very good question!

Privacy

If you are in business in the US, you have no right to privacy. That right only extends to you in the bathroom... unless of course you are under suspicion of a crime, in which case they can storm the restroom and take you by force. At any moment, a local agency can claim that you have been selected randomly for an audit. Audits can come from a variety of state or federal agencies. Many times it truly is random. However, in recent years, many suspect that auditing has been wielded like a weapon, specifically targeting certain businesses and organizations that go against political party agendas, the local boys club, or influential groups.

What is an audit? It's when a team of auditors show up on your doorstep to go through your books and review every aspect of your operation. They do this in an effort to ensure they've received their proper compensation and that you are properly reporting your income and the income of those who you contract with. They will literally follow the path of the money to you and from you – for every transaction. They will, of course, tell you that their process will not interrupt your operation, which is a total farce. I've been audited (without any issues, I might add...) by three different state agencies three different times, and it certainly was an inconvenience to daily business activities.

Beyond auditing, businesses also receive endless surveys from various agencies like the Census Bureau, the Department of Labor and Industries or Employment Security that demand that you fill out their forms so they can better tax and audit you. Very often, it ends in the development of a new tax or a higher tax rate because they found a trend that justifies a change. All the while, these individual agencies continue to grow out of control. These are the people whose income is based upon their performance as employees. Yet, somehow I get the feeling that I am working for *them*. Most of these taxes have nothing to do with whether or not a business has actually made any money. They are totally dependent upon employment and employment statistics. A company can be losing money and still owe taxes.

Back to the young couple hoping to open a restaurant. They will find themselves having to hire an accounting firm to do their monthly tax calculations for payroll, city business taxes and local occupational taxes. On top of this, they'll have the taxes on the utility entitlements.

Don't you wish you could go to another public agency and simply request a rate increase because you're expenses went up? That's what utility companies do. Think about it. The garbage, cable TV, power, water, and phone companies keep growing to serve an increasing number of clients and keep increasing their billing to us every year. Of course, the agencies that are approving these rate increases get their increase in the federal and local taxes that get tagged onto the bill along the way. How convenient.

As an independent business man, I would like to be able to pass all my increases onto my customers along the way. Businesses have to raise prices from time to time, but what usually happens instead is increased competition, putting increased pressure on profit margins. Company Z has opened down the street offering services at a slightly lower price, now I need to consider my pricing structure so I don't lose customers

How about the mandatory insurance you have to have to be in business? A great many business owners never use their required, hefty insurance coverage, but they have to have it! Government agencies even require that you have an extra "contractor's bond" for contracts over $300,000 when working on publicly-funded contracts in order to guarantee the job gets done. No extra coverage, no government contract. Of course, there are taxes on the insurance that benefits the insurance commissioner's office. Our young couple will soon find out about all the insurance they need for fire, casualty and liability. Each year when a policy renews, the rates start climbing, as do all the associated taxes. In many cases, it's the taxes that cause the rate increase.

I often think about my clients in the restaurant industry. Loading them down with all the information about government intervention up front would only serve to discourage them. I certainly don't want to chase away my clients and kill their dreams. For me, I constantly remind myself that I got into this business quite innocently, learning about the weight of government along the way. It was often alarming and sobering, and the weight has increased exponentially over the years. How convoluted and interdependent can we get? Let's talk about privatization.

What, a System With No Taxes?

I believe we need some organization and some controls, which will have costs associated with implementing them. So, just print it! Are you thinking that printing money will make what's already in circulation worth a little bit less? The amount of money in circulation has a relationship to the National GDP and the debt to asset ratio of our country. Once money is converted into real property or other assets, it comes out of circulation and becomes a part of the national assets. You have to print money in order to expand the economy. Some would say that it devalues the existing money, but it actually creates more room for business expansion. What causes the devaluation is inflation: the increased costs of goods, services, taxes, utilities, food, fuel, transportation, and housing. Adding more money to expand the economy does not in theory devalue what you have. Only the increased cost of what you spend it on does!

Let's track productivity, but not for the purposes of more taxes. How about tracking for analysis and to show levels of productivity and effectiveness? If the government needs more money, just print it and put it to good use rather than sending it abroad to pay off debt interest. We want our society to be productive and have a successful education system that works for all Americans. Our government prints a massive amount of money anyway. Let's not kid ourselves. It causes inflation. The government will always get what it needs in one way or the other. But, we can organize it and make it work for us if we want!

Necessity of Organization

I don't want to be critical of our systems and regulations and not acknowledge the need for organization. Obviously people can't be allowed to do anything they want whenever they want. The results would be chaotic and damaging. The proper perspective to have while creating the organization we need as a people is long-term vision. If we think long term, we come to the realization that we're each here for a short time. In the end, we really own nothing here on earth, only having temporary possession of things and property.

How we're organized as a society makes each country unique and hospitable. Knowing this planet extends far beyond our lifetimes, we also need to respect the environment.

But, how to find balance between maintaining controls without killing productivity is the key.

How do we implement controls without stifling the motivation of the entrepreneur? How do we maintain the infrastructure of society without over-taxing the very people who create the income and employ all the people?

Back in the late 50's, there was a book written by Ayn Rand called *Atlas Shrugged* that foretold the results of over-regulation and taxation by government. It was written in the form of a novel about the railroad and steel industries. Her insights were genius. When we reach the point when no one wants to be an employer any longer because the weight of governmental rules and regulations becomes too heavy, our society fails. The out-of-control growth of government causes immense inflation through their regulation, in turn causing products and services to become so expensive that our financial structure fails under the weight. The only answer is privatization...de-centralization.

Certain areas of our market would be better for everyone if they had more systems in place, and other areas would be better off less regulated. The competition found in free and open markets for goods and services has been the only way our society has been able to hold the line against inflation. Private companies come up with innovations that reduce operating costs to more competitively supply goods and services vs. what can be done under government control. Offer honest, competitive bidding to those who feel they have new cost-effective ways to approach and solve problems.

Unfortunately, we have government making rules that regulate the *way* they do business. These rules are most often the end result of special interest lobbying in the legislature. I have to ask the question, why do we allow these rules to be implemented? These rules and these groups, coupled with legislation they've advocated for, have now made America internationally uncompetitive in many industries.

There have always been as many special interest groups in our country as there are opinions. Generally, these groups represent workers for various industries in our society, such as labor unions. So many different unions exist, you can hardly count them. There's the electrical, plumbing, teamsters, automotive, teachers, and hospital workers, plus all of their associates. These unions have their lobbyists who work the legislature to level the playing field in regards to their entitlements. By *entitlements* I mean that the unions demand certain standards of benefits and wages for workers in these industries.

In order for a business or office to hire union workers as employees—and hope to stay in business in light of the weight of these benefits—the government imposes *prevailing wage standards* for publicly-funded projects and government contracts. Why? To make them competitive with non-union companies. Let me explain it this way: unions and the government have partnered, so when a non-union company could potentially satisfy a publicly-funded contract (do a job) less expensively, they won't let them. The result is that our government actually pays more for services than they would in a completely free and open market. I have to ask, is this a responsible way to spend the public's money? States already have workplace standards, employer rules and wage laws that all businesses must abide by. Can't we maintain performance and workplace standards without this additional, inflation-causing regulation?

I am not saying that union labor is not good labor. They are the best trained and educated workers in their fields. They have their own training and performance standards that insure people who hire these workers get quality work using the best state-of-the-art equipment. But, skill-building can certainly be done without any special legislation; apart from any "protective" group. Look at what's happening right now with our largest corporations—such as Boeing—that are controlled by large labor unions. The unions are actually controlling the costs to competitively produce products sold around the world, not Boeing itself. Boeing cannot compete against foreign competition for contracts, even within our own country's airlines because of these organized labor groups. We will continue to lose orders to European-based Air Bus until we take our plane manufacturing off-shore to escape all the added labor expenses.

We have priced ourselves out of our own jobs. I am sure the next move will be to pass government legislation to protect our Federal contracts from going overseas. But again, is this the right thing to do? Won't that just add more fuel to the fire?

Chapter Eight

THE WAR MACHINE
AND GOVERNMENT WASTE

When we talk about waste in government, we might think of over-staffing, $5000 toilet seats, and those expensive nights out for our politicians and their constituents. But, what about those decisions that affect all of us, that should not be our responsibility? There are so many things we could care less about, like certain commissioned studies. We all have our own stories and one for me involved my brother, Dennis.

Dennis had an attorney friend, Harold, who owned a little home on ten acres out in the country. Harold owned a number of properties that he rented out, this one included. He knew my brother was hurting for money, but was very handy with construction projects. He offered to let my brother occupy this country home if he slowly fixed it up while he lived there. This house needed just about everything you can imagine: plumbing, floors, paint, siding replacement, etc. Strangely, repairs also included the need to remove over one million tires that had been dumped on the property. *One million tires!*

As it turns out, the previous renter had a profitable business "recycling" old tires. In reality, this renter was just disposing of them, storing them up on Harold's property. This guy was a dishonest genius! He would go around to all the tire dealers and charge them a dollar a tire to dispose of them. He did this over a period of five years. Because the property was deep and narrow, he started back deep on the property and started piling up the tires in the weeds out of site. The house was situated up on the front of the property with the highway running in front of it. Just behind the house were two large barns which blocked the view of the back of the property from the road.

A number of years passed, and one of the neighbors finally complained about the unsightly piles of tires to the owner, who had no idea at all what was going on. Because this renter claimed he was a "tire farm" (is there even such a thing?) it took over a year to evict this renter. Evidently, there is a law that protects farmers from eviction due to their hardship. In some bizarre way, this guy fell into this classification. After he was successfully evicted, that's when my brother moved in to help with repairs and got a first-hand look at the craziness.

Because Harold was a savvy attorney, he always looked for technicalities to benefit his life and position. He found out about a state hazardous waste clean-up fund and made application to get the tax payers of the state to pay to clean up his property. His application was accepted for some reason, and the state hired a company to chip up the tires and recycle them into another program that used the waste to resurface highways. Now hear me…I do appreciate the need to clean up the planet, but not on private property, and not at *my* expense.

The previous renter was responsible for creating this mess. If all was fair in the world, he should have had to pay. So, what do you think about that? This was a state-level example, and we can only imagine the extent of this type of thing across the country. And, on the federal level, who is scrutinizing these expenditures and closely examining our budgets? No one asked me about spending my money in this way.

Control

Do our representatives really vote in the best interest of the American people as a whole? Look again at major issues like healthcare, education and military spending. How about our standing in the rest of the world? I'd like to have a say.

Today, our information networks are extensive. Via the internet, television, radio, phones, etc., every citizen can easily stay informed about major issues in debate.

Why don't we simply let the American people vote on all major issues of importance that affect our welfare? It's our money. Don't tell me the average citizen does not know what is going on in the world. Our media is very informative, and if you listen to programs like NPR, you can stay in tune with important political issues. I love the *pros and cons* format of debates. Give all the perspectives, facts and arguments, then simply let the people decide the outcome. We can be set up for both national and local issues. Keep it simple: the majority wins. Our representatives are too often affected by special interests.

What is the real issue here? Is it *control*? There will always be special interest groups. Right now, there is a great deal of control being wielded in Congress when it comes to spending on key issues. Often it has nothing to do with the will of the American people or the real needs of Americans. Those votes involve posturing and deals; deals made with regional special interests who'd benefit from the outcomes. Isn't the will, needs and care of Americans the most important issue? What do we really want? Do we need more fighter planes, or rapid transit in Seattle? Do we need more air tankers, or more healthcare insurance for Americans?

Our government has ultimate control over some of the largest sums of money in the world. With this money, our government is also running roughshod over the rest of the world. We have the largest and most powerful military in the world.

After 9-11, we went into Iraq for a second time even though many believe there was no connection between Osama Bin Laden and Iraq. Why in the world are we allowing this to happen? Is this our country? Or is it our government's wants and desires? Has the use of our military become about imperialism?

What about the control over the oil in Iraq? We all know this nation is dependent upon oil and that Iraq has one of the largest oil reserves under its deserts. There were probably no weapons of mass destruction like we were led to believe and no real justification for going after Iraq. Were we (or even our allies) in danger of being attacked by Iraq?

Let's face it, we cannot completely stop rogue groups of people from performing random acts of violence. These things are happening all around the world and are not specifically aimed at Americans. The people who have benefited by this attack on Iraq are the oil companies and all the military arms providers and contractors. These people are the benefactors of our spending and the decision to go to war with Iraq. Many people lost their lives. Was this even in the special interest of the Iraqi people; a people who have already been dealing with war and conflict for a thousand years? How many of their citizens have died? How much of the war money spent by our government has benefited the American citizens? Wouldn't we be better off implementing a new healthcare system for our country?

Are We Safe?

Is our country safe? No one in their right mind would ever think about a full-scale invasion of America. We have more guns here in our homes than any country in the world. If someone tried to invade American soil, we would immediately organize and take control like we did with the British Red Coats. However, with today's technology, someone could bring in some kind of bomb and set it off in a city or use some kind of chemical weapon against us. We can't stop this rogue behavior from people who act on their own. Any government official who says they can 100% protect us from some crazy person flying an airplane into a building is full of crap.

This is the same type of thing that has happened with school or movie theatre shootings. Some people are a few sandwiches shy of a full picnic, and they just go off. In a world with billions of people, sadly, these things are going to happen. We cannot fully stop this random behavior, and anyone who tells you they can is wrong. Cain killed his brother, Abel, with a rock. It's not about guns – it's about darkness in human hearts.

Even so, these random, destructive acts are *not* legitimate reasons to take away American freedoms. If you look at the legislation that has been passed in the years since 9-11, we have systematically lost most of our freedoms to categorical manipulation and justification. We may actually need protection from our own government, especially when it comes to how they're destroying us financially.

Terrorist threats are used as an excuse to fund the U.S. military war machine efforts. I am not sure I believe anything shown on the news anymore or the skew in which things are presented to us. We hear justifications for our military wanderings around the planet. Although, I imagine there've been scores of secret missions and fronts the general public are clueless about in the last decade. Who really knows the truth about how many people from other countries have been killed due to our involvement. Is there really anyone that represents our feelings about these invasions?

So, are we safe? Yes, as safe as any country can be that shares borders and is technologically savvy. We have enough fire power to destroy the world several times over. We could decide tomorrow to destroy any country we wanted to if they threatened us. Why then do we keep building our military and keep interfering in other countries' affairs? Are we doing it to keep up with the military Joneses, so-to-speak? Maybe *we are* the Joneses and like to flex our muscles. I believe these are the real things that threaten our safety. Is all this really in the best interest of the American people?

Some politicians would say it is in order to justify their behavior. Or, is it really the way our government is spending money that's creating a threat to our economic welfare around the world? At this point in time, we are far more threatened economically than militarily. We have allowed our government to control our money far too long. They are using it to influence power around the world instead of spending it here on our soil. This is becoming the biggest threat to the American way of life. We don't need any more weapons of mass destruction any more than Iraq did in the 90's.

Switzerland has something figured out. What if we were

like Switzerland: neutral and peaceful. We could certainly protect our shores and promote peace around the world instead of invading other countries. Frankly, I don't know why we haven't put some of our leaders in jail for misleading the American people to justify the invasion of Iraq. Being thought of as a peaceful nation around the world will do more to promote peace than our current situation.

De-centralization

If you look casually at our governmental system, we have a tremendous amount of duplication. If we look at the way our society is organized, we have our national branches of military which exist in most states. There's the FBI and the CIA. We have our state police, our county sheriff's departments and also the police in each city of our country. Now, how much control do we need? How many jurisdictions do we need?

When we look around the world, America has 662 military bases in strategic locations. The list is so long it would take up pages. Do we want to continue to finance the policing of the world, or be a part of an international coalition of nations (like the United Nations) that monitors global activities? I say it would be wise to cut back our international presence and spend our money on *our* people. We need only to protect our borders and have a strong national defense. As I indicated earlier in this book, many in this country have a gun or two in their homes, and our military already has enough fire power to blow the world up several times over. Why don't we become a peaceful nation that takes care of our own?

Our government has been demonstrating *abuse of power* to the world. We have put too much power in the hands of too few people. When you consider the size of the US economic machine, it is mind boggling. Like the universe, it is ever expanding. We have social security, federal unemployment tax and the income tax systems. It has now reached a total average of 35% of everyone's gross wages. This means that every working man, woman and youth works over one third of their working life to support government.

We have the most powerful economy in the world, and the main benefactor is our federal government. Think about it. Other than protecting our country, what direct benefit do we receive from our federal government?

Our government officials receive plenty, including pensions, nearly free healthcare, security teams (which I completely understand) and pay. But, why should they have special entitlements and better programs that *we* have to pay for?

The people of this country should decide exactly what we want from our government on a federal level, and then fund it from the state government level, having states collect all income taxes. By doing it this way, we can take control over how money is spent and eliminate all the duplication and control the government has over citizens.

Weapons of Mass Expense

Legislators have too much power over our money and how it's spent. Don't you think continuing to spend billions on military contractors and weapons (at an unprecedented level) is insane? These contractors like Grumman and Boeing are always trying to get the next big contract through insider influence.

When I think of the $750 billion that our government has spent on Middle East peacekeeping efforts and the money spent on building more weapons, it makes me ill. Who is keeping the United States in check for developing too many weapons of mass destruction? Is this what the American people want for themselves and their children? I say that our government has grown out of control because it uses the collective power of Americans' hard work to enforce its moral will on the world. The result is financial oppression and emotional depression.

Why do we have this war mentality? Isn't it the United States today that is fueling the growing military build-up by sticking our noses where they don't belong? As long as we maintain this insane military attitude, our world will never be at peace. We need to decentralize this war-making power and let the people of America decide how they want to spend their money, how they want to be perceived in the world, and stop letting so few people decide what we're going to do politically around the world.

The fault today lies with our outdated party system used to manipulate the power and control the people. They have systematically taken away our power and choices and have treated us like children who need to be babysat.

Our government has proven to us that they're irresponsible with our money and the power it brings. They should not be trusted with making decisions that don't directly benefit the people (us) providing the money. I believe most people are more fearful about losing freedoms in this country versus being invaded by another nation. So, why does all this madness continue? If we are such a peaceful nation, why are we the leader of building bombs and the great military fighting machine? If we are peaceful, why don't we spend money on being peaceful? The people of this nation are the most charitable people in the world, but our government is not spending the bulk of its monies on peaceful things. What if we kept our noses out of other people's business?

There is an old school thought process preventing us from holstering our weapons. Are there dangers in the world? Yes. Are there dangerous nations in the world? Yes, there is the potential for great danger. So, who is finally going to put down their gun first and decide not to fight anymore?

> There is an old school thought process preventing us from holstering our weapons.

It is clear to me that other world powers exploit the power money brings to build military might. This whole thought process of building an intimidating arsenal is confrontational behavior in itself. Old school thinking says that doing this is *preventive* behavior. Protecting our people and nation is important, but is the extent of all of this really the will of the people? Not only *no*, but *hell no*!

Chapter Nine

THE ECONOMY AND
THE EVOLUTION OF BUSINESS

What do we want from government? First, we want government to be run responsibly by the wishes of *the people.*

Being run *responsibly* also means managing the government within the revenue being generated by the economy. How is it that 47 states and the federal government are broke? It is funny how degrees and higher education are so valued. In government, we seek out the well-educated people and put them into positions of power and authority, yet none of them are getting it right. Is the education they received teaching them about what the real world really needs? I'm not convinced. With all these educated lawmakers, why can't we simply balance the budget anymore?

Our system no longer works. We don't have anyone out there now advocating changes that will help the majority of people. Special interest groups are wreaking havoc.

Ask yourself: what is *my* special interest as an American citizen? I suspect it has more to do with getting opportunities, general welfare and safety.

Questions like, is our country safe? Or, do we have a good healthcare system? Is our infrastructure like roads and our educational system in good shape? These should be the root issues concerning America today. What is it that we are currently doing with our tax dollars? How did this thing get so far out of control and government get so large?

Speaking of Large...

As I write this in 2015, our latest president and Congress passed the largest financial stimulus package in American history. This package was passed by a small group of people (535) who are supposed to be acting on behalf of 320 million Americans. According to the ever-changing National Debt Clock, of these 320 million, less than one third (97 million Americans) work and support the entire system. By the time you read this, those numbers will no doubt be even more disparaging.

I don't see how this stimulus package did anything beneficial other than helping the people who've already been systematically taking from the majority of people in this country. Why would we give money to a banking system that is not working? We have asked the auto makers to present a re-organization plan to Congress to justify the bail-out money, but why haven't we asked the bankers to do the same?

Let's keep in mind that the federal government makes and monitors the banking regulations. Unless the regulations are changed, the bankers cannot give the money to people who need it, because they don't qualify under their own regulations! The truth is that banks are taking these homes from people, and they now have *bad paper* (foreclosed loans) that makes them insolvent just like any other failing company. So, we are going to give them our money to make them solvent again, and they also get to take our homes and put people out on the street? What?

Government Loyalty to Their Own Communities

When we started our business 29 years ago, my brother and I registered with the state, county and city government agencies in order to bid on local projects and to become a contracted vendor. Things went well for many years, and we averaged about $25K to $50K per month with the State of Washington Department of Corrections. We also did well with the Thurston County Jail. Then, everything changed with the internet.

The State Legislature voted to always go with the lowest bid when securing service and product contracts, and not just getting bids from local companies, but through national bidding. As soon as their electronic bidding system went live, we no longer got this business. This also meant we were suddenly competing with out-of-state dealers and other businesses outside of our local economy. These dealers are a part of large national buying groups who can purchase equipment and supplies at better wholesale pricing. So, my state's spending went out of state and my business lost income opportunities. Take the money out of the flow in this community and what happens? We lose the pebble in the pond effect.

> There is no loyalty any longer to keep money in our own communities.

Before, when they would purchase with in-state vendors, those vendors would deal with other local vendors, in turn causing the money ripple effect that has a very large, positive effect on the economy. There is no loyalty any longer to keep the money in our own communities. Who is it that is making these short-sighted decisions? Not very wise, long-term! Why don't we keep our tax dollars in our local economy?

It reminds me of the story for the federal bid for refueling tankers that Boeing and Airbus both bid on...and Boeing lost! I think it was Patty Murray that stood up and shut down that contract because the feds were about to award the contract to Airbus. It is really no different when on a smaller scale we place hundreds of orders for goods and services out of state or out of the country that add up to millions of dollars. Again the ripple effect of removing these dollars from our local or national economy has a far-reaching effect on employment and tax revenues. We should not allow those who represent us to continue to serve when they make decisions like these!

Crazy Businesspeople
You want to start a business? You Must be Crazy!

Okay, Mr. President, you think you know how to help the American people and get business going again? Let's talk about solving the problem. The weight of government *is* the problem. I am talking about the weight of government on every level: state, county, city, and federal.

The tax burden is out of control on every level of our society, and the tax burden is what causes inflation and stress on businesses. Don't assume businesses can handle it, especially considering the increased competition. In business, we fight to maintain margins for our businesses to survive and to pay our employees, let alone have anything left for bombs and wars. Let's cut inflation by reducing our spending. Let's get rid of all the special departments and get down to the basic needs of Americans.

Stop taxing my business and taking the money to spend it overseas on stuff that isn't affecting my safety and well-being. Stop building bombs that we don't need. Don't tell me we need to update our arsenal of weapons and develop more weapons to try and control the world.

Business taxes are counterproductive to employment. If people are employed, then the employer collects and pays income tax to the federal government. Personal income tax is far more productive than taxing the businesses in America. And, if I own the business, tax my pay, not the business itself. If that were the case, I could pay myself and my employees more.

The list of government expenses drives government taxation, and that chokes business growth and development. It's time to take a microscope and examine the extent and ramifications of government expenses and rules, and allow business to operate and reinvest profits in goods, services and people instead.

The Free Market Economy and Capitalism

We use the political terms *socialism, capitalism,* and *communism*. People tend to want to label all of our little discoveries or even the most miniscule of behaviors. Creating labels and boxes for everything isn't always helpful. Things aren't always one way or the other, nor do they fall neatly into given categories. The worst thing we can do when talking philosophically is to generalize, categorize or name a group or action based upon past human behavior or history. There is no time in history like today nor will there be another time period exactly the same in the future. Circumstances will always be different. There is no clear, statistical relationship between our economic woes today and the crash of 1929. The sheer population numbers and the magnitude of the dollars involved are very different, and so are the technological differences. So, as we look at our situation today and talk about free markets and capitalism, we need only to consider the circumstances of today.

Capitalism is when people are allowed to create diversified work for themselves through the sale of products or services for a profit. The object is to find a need for a product or service and fill that need. When you've identified your product or service, traditionally the "market" is where you'd sell or trade it (farmer's market, shopping malls, local real estate markets, stock market, etc.). We prefer to do this profitably!

With the growing number of people in the world, there is no shortage of consumers. Whatever the market, there's bound to be a large number of customers. There are three types of markets: emerging markets for new products, mature markets, and dying markets of all types. The question today is regarding the maturity of the markets and the amount of providers of the goods and services. Every market has a lot of providers and customers. Are there enough consumers to support the number of providers in a particular market? Is there a growing market for that product or service? There are limited markets for some products (cemetery plots) and continuous markets for others (food). In order to have a healthy national economy, we need continuous growth in the majority of our markets. Unhealthy, flat, declining markets will see declining prices and profits.

What happens when a market slows down? The

competition gets tight and we start fighting over the same loaf of bread. Profits get tight and there is a fallout of competitors. This is when businesses start to go under. They say that only the strong survive, but when our population gets to the level that it is, does the face of the world market change when one area fails? At a time when we are trying to bring the whole world together, does competition in the free market divide us?

It used to be that America was the only capitalist society. During the Cold War, when ideological differences divided us, the communist world ridiculed our way of life. Now, the whole world seems to be after personal wealth and all the technological toys. We all want the same standard of living around the world. But, what happens when all these markets mature at the same time and inflation, due to greed, literally chokes the markets?

I pointed out in an earlier chapter that inflation has changed the budgets of American families, but it is also true around the world. People everywhere strive to have the comforts of life, while the manufacturers and distributors of those products strive to meet their own needs along the way. The results are massively inflated prices, and sooner or later, no one can afford to purchase these items. The housing market is a perfect example. There is no room at the bottom of the market for young families to purchase a home on entry-level incomes. When the bottom is no longer accessible, it falls out, and the whole thing comes to a halt! This is where we find the weakness in our capitalist society.

Where greed meets stunted growth, capitalism fails. Where does the majority of greed lie? Once again, I go back to the banking system. Someone that brokers loans once told me that we can't have loans direct to the people from the government because they don't have the infrastructure in place to process the lending program. Wait...I say the Fed already has an organization that polices the banking system, literally checking all their loans and documentation to ensure they meet federal lending regulations. A moderate

> *Where greed meets stunted growth, capitalism fails.*

increase in staff would eliminate the middle man and free up more money, opening up the housing markets again.

The World Economy

Over the past 30 years, the world's economy has been evolving. Developing nations around the world have benefitted, especially those nations where American companies have exported technology and jobs. Business leaders in America have found it cost effective to manufacture products off shore in less expensive labor markets. There are pros and cons to this change.

While this has been good to reduce the price of goods, it has taken manufacturing jobs from American soil and American workers. Now that these nations have the technology, they are competing against us for market share, causing a decline in all other job-related categories. This has collectively reduced our market share in the industries that we originated and previously dominated. The airline, semi-conductor and automotive industries are prime examples. This inter-dependent relationship around the world now affects us together. When our stock market turns down, so do the European and Asian markets. We've become locked together and in competition with one another. World markets mature together, and we are now dealing with mature markets and fierce competition. Manufacturing regulations, increased taxes, union requirements, and environmental legislation all play a role in increased pricing that's put the cost of luxury items like cars, boats and homes out of reach for many. Cars and homes didn't used to be luxury items – most working families could easily afford them. We need some real changes real quick in order to turn the tide.

Chapter Ten

PIECES, BITS AND MORE IDEAS

What happens when the population's needs are greater than the ability of the economy to produce enough revenue to take care of everyone? Right now, this is not only happening, but it is happening within many governments – ours and throughout the world. A capitalist society is based upon continuous consumption on the part of a growing population. This system fails when we reach a level where there is no longer disposable income in most families' budgets.

We are now finding that inflation has devoured disposable income for the basic things we need to live: food, electricity, gas, water, sewer, property taxes, healthcare insurance, auto insurance, home owners insurance, cable, garbage, recycling, and gasoline. While public utilities commissions keep approving the fleecing of the public in order to maintain the standard of living and profitability of these companies and employees, the American public is growing poorer year after year. This is where we are losing the middle class.

Although your thought process may reject the next idea I'm about to suggest, think it through for a moment. I advocate that the public no longer pays for health and utility-related items. I suggest that they should be provided because they are basic needs of every person. The public, the people, should own the utility companies that provide these vital services. We can still have private companies and people could still help fund operations in some way, but our system simply must change. It is failing and leaving a lot of people behind.

We need a new system and a new philosophy based upon living a quality life, and if every philosophy has to have a name, then let's call this one *socapism*.

"Socapism"

This new philosophy would take the for-profit aspect out of services for certain foundational needs of the people. Utility companies and health services would be provided based upon the needs of the population and the need to support the infrastructure that provides those needs. This system would also create jobs to grow the infrastructure to keep up with demand.

World resources should belong to the world, not individuals or individual companies that profit from their ownership. It is absurd to think that an individual owns the oil of the planet, or the gold, diamonds, gas, or the coal. These are nature's elements that God provided for us to sustain the life on this planet. Everything is already divided up and so few have so much, yet I've heard that as many as 500 million people go to bed starving every night. These people have no food or adequate shelter. If we made them strong and helped establish systems for meeting their basic needs, they could help clean up the planet and make it healthy again. Education is the great equalizer that will help pull large parts of impoverished countries out of their problems; education, resources and opportunity.

Shifting the Status Quo

All this being said, it's easier said than done! This kind of transformation starts out as a challenge for our mindsets. We've had things the way they are for so long, it is very difficult for people to change their perspective. That reminds me of the problems in Iraq. When the U.S. attempted to help Iraq establish a democratic system, we saw how difficult it is to get people to agree...if ever. This is another reason why we need leaders who are centered in faith, not their own greed. Men that struggle for power and control for their personal gain need to be taken out of politics – at all levels. People who are in positions of leadership need to come together in agreement and solution now or be replaced by honest, true representatives of the people.

Can there be a global shift in thinking? Yes, it can happen and can be instituted *if* it is the true will of the people. As the people, we must come together and desire and demand it. We need to replace manipulative leaders with people that are interested in preservation and representing the needs of the people they serve.

The United Nations is a perfect example of an international coalition of government that was established for the people... all people. I believe this guiding collaboration started out with good intentions for peace and solutions, but once again we have political posturing based upon the current mantra of the ruling party within the given countries. We need to recognize the rights of all people, regardless of their culture or country of origin. We don't need to agree on everything or conform to one way of living, but certain issues in the world require agreement and collaboration. We need leaders that are exhibiting the fruit of the Spirit of God, and who operate with love and kindness, not greed.

I see the value in government providing healthcare, shelter, work opportunities, and education. Not all people are equal in their abilities to learn and work, but everyone has something beneficial to contribute. People should still be financially rewarded based upon their level of contribution and skill.

We can turn this around now. We have the United Nations that needs to institute some ground rules based upon the immediate needs of preservation. Why can't we as one society print money based upon an individual's contribution and ensure that we are all working for the good of a unified society rather than a divided world?

Public or Private?

Organization at some level is good in order to keep our society from falling into chaos, but should the services that we require be privately owned or for-profit corporations? Should the utilities that we all require be publicly owned by all the people? I say yes! Let us own the phone, cable, garbage, water, and power companies.

Who is funding the demands of growth today? What's the cost of providing services to the public for the various utilities we all require? What is the true level of profits that the current companies operating the utilities have? Utility companies are applying to the Public Utilities Commission for rate increases at an alarming pace. We see staggering increases, between 10-25% per year. Can people afford to have utility bills the size of mortgages? With increases continuing, we'll get there eventually. Are we all paying for the growing infrastructure for these companies or are the contractors? If all of us owned it, then great – let's collaboratively support the infrastructure's expansion. But, if it's a for-profit entity...pay for it yourself! And, who is minding the bank? We must remember these are *for-profit* corporations that are getting a little bit from all of us.

When we consider the current cost of basic services and the rate at which they've collectively increased, we can clearly see where our disposable income has gone! The American people want to live a relaxed life without all the unnecessary stress caused by out-of-control financial demands. So, what are the people that represent us doing to help *mainstream America*?

Get a Job

Everyone should have a job! Everyone should contribute in some meaningful way. Let's say there is a mother at home who is single, has three kids and can't work because she has no childcare. She can get assistance, but is provided childcare training to take care of other children in order to continue on assistance. No free rides.

Everyone contributes in whatever way they can. If there is a person with drug or alcohol problems, they will be given care, but if they choose not to straighten up, they will go to rehabilitation of an appropriate kind. No free rides for anyone. Many of us have higher levels of education, and would not be fulfilled unless we were able to pursue our chosen professions and areas of giftedness.

In the Bible, Jesus tells a story called *the parable of the talents* and recognizes the stewardship capacity and skill level of three different men. Each individual has their own abilities and capabilities. In free-market societies, everyone has a level of financial productivity based upon their education, natural abilities, level of ambition or chosen profession. Even in an international government you can establish levels of compensation for different areas or work from scientists to laborers that work with the utility companies.

There are far too many people sitting around doing nothing; people who could be providing work that will improve our society and provide a level of dignity for the individual. Why do we even have unemployment? There must be *something* beneficial they can do rather than get free money for nothing. Why don't we put unemployed people to work fixing roads, cleaning up the community or assisting teachers and give them a "reemployment" pay check for doing so? Why should we pay unemployment dollars to someone for sitting at home? Many people could be employed to simply clean up communities, or to help re-establish the ecosystem by planting trees or maintaining our transportation systems. Let's put the unemployment money (and the unemployed) to work.

As long as a person is willing to work, why not give them something meaningful to do and pay them for it. Don't tell me we don't need new roads, sewers, farms, dams, and hospitals!

Just Go Ahead and Print It

If you put money into circulation, it will just keep moving, so just go ahead and print what we need to keep people in a productive system. Unfortunately, extra money being printed now goes towards paying off interest on loans we have with other countries, like China, and not into *our* system. But, if it was coming into our system, we could all do business with one another and keep the money moving.

All we each need is *enough*. Why not improve people's

knowledge so they can contribute to society by making higher education free? Why not figure out a way to fund viable business plans that's easier and more accessible than what the SBA offers now? Make it easy and affordable to loan the restaurant owner the money needed to establish their business. Loan the printer the money to purchase the printing press for their business. Right now money is too hard to get because banks and lending institutions are afraid to take a risk. Take away the risk, and give money to those who need it to get people employed and productive. If companies need more money to employ more people, subsidize them in some measured way. Yes, there needs to be some controls and limits, but what does it matter, as long as we all get a relative standard of living based upon our contribution and abilities?

And, what's wrong with price fixing for certain products? Look at what has happened to the cost of healthcare insurance. Even if you have it, it no longer covers or protects you and your family one hundred percent. If we all sell at the same price, no one individual company can control a market. All we need is enough to enjoy life for the short time we are here.

So, You Think You Own Something?

I would like to remind everyone on the planet that we are all just passing through. God owns everything not us! We are only stewards with temporary possession. Our government has taken ownership of all real property through perpetual taxation which has risen out of control. They also control the funding sources to purchase what we have been calling *our* homes. They use these taxation and fundraising programs to perpetuate their entitlements and life styles.

I would think hard about trapping yourself into the misguided perception of ownership of any type of property in todays' economy. Unless some major reform measures are put into effect, the government will continue to tax people out of their homes to perpetuate their own best interests. If you honestly compare the cost of home ownership today (including all the tax and insurance requirements) to renting you will often find that you can actually save more money by renting.

The days of massive increased valuations of homes are gone! People are actually losing more equity and ending up owing more than the property is worth in today's market. I would only suggest purchasing property if you can pay cash for it. Owning property free and clear is a good move for retired people today who are on fixed, low incomes. Owning your home means your only housing expenses are taxes and insurance, and occasionally a few repairs. Most people can at least afford to pay their taxes, which are generally lower than rent costs.

Our Infrastructure

As I travel around the country on business or for vacation, I can't help but use our nation's Interstate highway system. In each state, there are certain highways that are designated "federal," initially created by Dwight D. Eisenhower to be used for commerce and defense purposes. These should be the finest roads in our country, but no, they are not. Most of them are over 50 years old.

Over the past 35 years, I've noticed the roads have slowly deteriorated. Quite often, I use Interstate 5 in Washington State, and the road between Olympia and Seattle will beat your car to death. It has been that way for the past 20 years, and I wonder why we haven't allocated enough money from our tax dollars to address this and other public transportation systems in our major cities. If we keep delaying, it undoubtedly keeps getting more expensive.

There's no doubt we need good roads, but subsidizing car manufacturers and oil companies? This continued support of the automotive and oil industries in our country is madness. Everyone knows the world is going to run out of oil at some point. Long-term thinking is necessary and should get us started moving in another direction. By severing our allegiance to oil and embracing updated technologies, our major cities' transportation systems could take on a different look.

Seattle is one of the top five worst traffic-jammed cities in America. The area is gridlocked because the city is sandwiched between the Puget Sound to the west and Lake Washington to the east. We badly need mass transit running 20 miles north and south of the city. We can't ever seem to agree on how best to take action, and all the while the problem keeps getting worse.

Visit London or Paris – their rail systems are incredible and efficient. They are used extensively, daily, and they work very well. What if we took some of the money we spend on weapons of mass destruction and war and reallocate some of it to fix our infrastructure? It really could be that simple. Instead of paying people to make bombs, we can pay people to build good, rapid transit systems that run from the suburbs to the cities.

Aside from local school district levies, no one has asked me how I'd like my tax dollars to be spent. Why can't the

American peop_e vote cn the big issues?

Healthcare

Michael Moore, a famous (or infamous) advocate of national healthcare, traveled around the world and asked international citizens about their various, government-run programs. You might remember Michael from his DVD called *Sicko* about our healthcare system. In general, he found that people in other countries absolutely loved the programs and that most of their needs were being met.

Some time ago, I was on a ski trip in British Columbia, Canada, and suddenly had appendicitis. I ended up in a BC hospital and received fantastic care from the Canadian healthcare system. The funny thing is, my US insurance company tried to deny the surgeon's bill because he worked for the BC healthcare system. I had to file a claim with the Insurance Commissioner at the State of Washington to get them to pay the bill. After two years, it was finally resolved. The man who saved my life was finally paid in full. This is a real-life example of why for-profit programs (like insurance companies) don't belong in this healthcare industry. To them, profitability comes before doing what's right.

What do you want from your healthcare system? For me, I want the best care I can get when I need it the most. I want that for my friends and family, too. This is contrary to the objective of the average healthcare insurance company, which is in business to make profits. Denying claims and people *not* getting care is good for their bottom line. Oftentimes, our US healthcare providers have claims representatives who routinely deny coverages to increase their profitability.

Critical, preventative procedures such as angiograms, which might reveal major problems, are prescribed as a last resort because of cost.

What happens to all the insurance premiums we pay out? Looking at the Canadian system, working Canadians pay about $70 per month for healthcare. If every working American paid into a national system, we could significantly reduce our individual costs. I myself am paying $450 per month for coverage, which ten years ago was better coverage and cost me $250. Not only has the cost doubled and the coverage reduced, now I also have an annual deductible of $1000. Let's do the math...Canadians $70 and Americans $450. What about the stress caused in our society by having to make a healthcare payment that's the size of a second house payment? The existing system is reducing the quality of life for the American people, and only the lower and middle class feel the slap of it.

The solution is to have a national premium like the Canadian system. Everyone pays if they have a job, and even those who receive unemployment have their premium automatically paid out of that check. If a person wanted premium or selective coverage, they could purchase extra coverage as desired, just like in Canada. Eliminate the for-profit section of the coverage. The only negative I've heard about Canada's system is when a specialist is needed, sometimes there are longer wait times for procedures. Making medicine an attractive career and educating and training more doctors will resolve that issue.

I believe the systems that influence the quality of life of the masses should be owned and operated by the masses. This healthcare idea is not socialism, because you still have to purchase the coverage from your income. No one is asking for anyone to give it to us free. We are only asking to have it provided at a reasonable cost and to have a good scope of coverage.

SUMMARY AND WHAT'S NEXT

Although I have some ideas, I certainly don't have all the answers. Things are much more complex when we start considering the human dynamics in government. Within the structure of government, it seems like little kingdoms have been built; kingdoms that exist to monitor or babysit some segment of the private sector. Notice all the agencies we have which are nothing more than watch dogs for some segment of publicly-funded programs. They lobby for support in state and federal legislative circles. Why do we need all this? Why has it become so complicated? We have created these monsters that need to be fed. The weight of it all is killing the spirit of the people who create the businesses that support it all.

The working citizen is the support of the entire infrastructure of this country, and somehow, regulations and taxes keep piling on to the point that no one could possibly know all the rules.

My hope is that people can enjoy their lives more and have more free time for themselves and their families. I want to see families stay together, not being torn apart by the need to pursue money and support government instead of the family unit. Each person needs work of some kind. We should all work and have enough left to live and enjoy life and our loved ones. Healthcare is a priority, not world domination. We should be concerned about our people and families, first. I want to see mothers have the opportunity to stay at home and raise their children, rather than indifferent day cares. I want to see the average American person be able to afford a car and a home. I don't think a person should lose their home if they get sick.

There are major problems in our society and government, and they aren't getting any better. Let's stop being so passive. It's time to get involved and be the voices of change.

This book is my way of not just sitting around and complaining about things. I feel the need to express my opinions and those of my friends and colleagues. Perhaps this can serve as the beginning of a new way of thinking and of the people coming back together.

We don't want any more compromises. We don't want any more broken promises. We want to see the results of real change on our behalf. Let's start focusing on things at home first, and then be a part of world efforts to address international problems. It's time to recognize that we cannot afford to continue doing things the way we have done them in the past.

Dismantling the Monster

Now that the economy has come to a grinding halt, we need to start dismantling the monster. We need real accountability. The public needs to know what's really in the Federal Budget. The budget takes up volumes of books; books that can fill an entire room.

The big question is how do we go about organizing change that the people want? We have a lot of government people that don't want change, because it threatens their existence and control. It reminds me of the Pharisees when Jesus came. They decided to kill Him to protect their seat of power. They loved their rules more than the truth.

So, how do we get this out to vote on it? Let's take it step by step, starting with a couple simple things like the party system and the Electoral College. If we allow the government to pay for the election costs and give all candidates an equal public voice with (no party affiliation) they can run purely on issues! Eliminate the Electoral College and let the straight popular vote determine the outcome. No more primaries manipulated by the parties. Partisanship has proven itself as a blockage to progress. The people that represent the people should represent the people, *not a party* and party position.

Coming Elections

In the coming elections, I encourage the American people to *vote out* all incumbent party-affiliated candidates and *vote in* all independent representatives as our voice of change. We need to shake up the system, and then have our new representatives put forth these changes to help take back our country!

That's All, Folks

I'm just an ordinary man who has lived in this country for 63 years. I have paid all my taxes. I have voted. I have strived for the American dream. I've begun to notice the quality of life slipping away from the American people due to over-taxation and regulation.

I am not affiliated with any party or group, I am just an American. I've voted for Republicans, Democrats and

Independents before. There will no doubt be some who'll want to label me in unrealistic ways and tear down these ideas. People who are fiercely attached to the status-quo will plan those attacks. I understand. The box they're stuck in isn't quickly shed.

Thank you for reading *The New Revolution*. Share it with others. I hope it sparks discussions that lead to new solutions. By writing this book, I've said what I am compelled to share and have done what I set out to do: share a new perspective and inspire Americans to rethink our systems.

You're invited to join the discussion at Larry Backstrom's Facebook page or at www.TheNewRevolution.website.

About the Author

Businessman Larry Backstrom was born in Milwaukee, Wisconsin, in 1951. Mr. Backstrom spent his formative years on chicken and hops farms in Oregon. At the age of 18, he moved to the Bay Area to attend college. For six years, he attended three junior colleges, studying both pre-med and business.

After his education, Mr. Backstrom entered the electronics industry, working as a purchasing manager for a control system manufacturer. In 1975, he was offered a position with Avnet, the largest electronic component distributor in the world. As the division operations manager, he learned the distribution industry. He was appointed regional manager of operations on the West Coast and served on a corporate committee as an advisor to corporate operations decisions.

In 1979 Mr. Backstrom was recruited, with two other industry professionals, to open a division for Schweber Electronics in the Bay Area. He was appointed the product marketing director and director of operations of the division. The division quickly grew to over 180 employees and went from being the 125th largest distributor in gross sales to the third largest distributor, with sales in excess of 60 million dollars in 1985.

Personally, in 1983, Mr. Backstrom had his first child and soon after made the decision to leave the Bay Area for the Pacific Northwest in order to raise their daughter around his extended family. He moved to Olympia, Washington, where he started Olympic Food Equipment Sales in 1986 with his brother, Dennis.

The Backstrom brothers worked as partners successfully for 25 years until Dennis's retirement in 2010. Mr. Backstrom still owns and operates Olympic Food Equipment Sales, Inc., designing and building commercial food service facilities.

Mr. Backstrom has been working in the distribution industry for the past 40 years and has learned about business and government throughout his career. Most of the opinions expressed in this book have come as a result of working in and managing multi-million dollar distribution operations. His work with some of the largest corporations in America in the semi-conductor and food service equipment industries has shaped his opinions and understanding of business in America today.

The New Revolution is proudly published by:

Creative Force Press

www.CreativeForcePress.com

Do You Have a Book in You?